T0381400

DIVERSITY WORKFORCE
MEMOIR
GLOBAL DEMAND FOR
AUTHENTIC LEADERSHIP

JAMES F. S. SEEKIE, SR.
LEARNER PhD
MA INTERNATIONAL BUSINESS

AuthorHouse™
1663 Liberty Drive
Bloomington, IN 47403
www.authorhouse.com
Phone: 1 (800) 839-8640

This book is printed on acid-free paper.

ISBN: 978-1-7283-1409-9 (sc)
ISBN: 978-1-7283-1410-5 (e)

Print information available on the last page.

Published by AuthorHouse 06/17/2020

authorHOUSE®

TABLE OF CONTENTS

CHAPTER I

CHAPTER II

CHAPTER III

CHAPTER IV

CHAPTER V

TABLES INDEX

FOREWORD

The Team leadership role and unconscious bias treatment at the coffee shop in Philadelphia, in 2018, reflects the deficit of Diversity Inclusion (D&I), under the Affirmative Action. The *CAFÉ SHOP's* incident involving implicit bias treatment of a *"BLACKMAN"* is a reawaken call for more engagements of the dialogue about diversity inclusion. Leadership deficit challenges diversity inclusion across organizations like coffee shops and other workplaces as governmental, private, and international organizations, including the fortune 500 corporations, among others. Organizations are challenged by the intercultural leadership deficit gap for managers required to provide intercultural competent authentic leadership (ICAL) at a global scale to remain competitive. The deficit includes intercultural incompetence that needs attention over the next decade as globalization challenges organizational management to maintain operational performance equilibrium. The intercultural competence gap to balance operational services will involve strategic planning for diversity inclusion and appropriate training for leaders and managers.

THE PURPOSE OF THE BOOK

The purpose of this book is to increase awareness of Diversity Team Leadership (DTL), conscious and unconscious bias (UB) synergy through information and education, to overcome the challenges of diversity workplaces. A leadership deficit is among organizations, including the Fortune 500 corporations, the nonprofit sectors, and governmental organizations at a cost. The book explains the need for diversity Team intercultural competence for the management of organizations as an innovation, reflecting workforce culture. It provides a synopsis about strategic planning for diversity inclusion roadmap for Federal, State, Nonprofits, and Profit corporations (local and international).

AFTERWORDS

The book discusses diversity inclusion from the lens of organizational human capital strategic planning management and the role of the inclusive workforce for productivity and efficiency. The correlation between diversity workforce and Teamwork in the governmental or non-governmental organizations and the ability to have an excellent occupational health operation in organizational management is analyzed.

The incident at the coffee shop unconscious bias treatment became a national narrative about the deficits of Affirmative Action. The book examines the need for diversity education to overcome the barriers to underrepresentation at workplaces to enable diversity inclusion. The role of the US Congressional watchdog Management Directive (MD715) for Affirmative Action remains watchful as it monitors diversity inclusion to support an inclusive and balanced diverse workplace.

ACKNOWLEDGEMENT

My Teamwork experience and encounters with the global diversity environment began in Banking, Government, Nonprofit sectors, and after attending several international events, including the Trade Fair in Milan, Italy. The event was a contribution of what has become globalization as international communication and technology changed to a new direction after the industrial revolution. At the time, participants attending the Fair were asked to use the conference earphones and listen to their languages through interpreters. The conference occurred during a period the EU was becoming one of the regional economic Trade partners with most regions, including African economies.

Interaction with participants of European and international businesses was preceded by attending Banking Economics Conference in Lagos, Nigeria, involving several Banking institutions in Africa. Studies and Alumni connection includes: The World council of credit Union in Canada, the International Cooperative Alliance ICA, Geneva, Israeli cooperative system, and First National City Bank (FNCB) Alumnus, Now Citibank, New, York, and global monetary systems Study of African, Caribbean, Pacific Trade (ACPs), European Union and North America Free Trade (NAFTA), US Foreign Direct Investment (FDI) in food globally, and the Brazilian economy.

The International Trade Fair occurred after the theory of Globalization was coined by a Hungarian Theorist in 1960, advancing the call for globalization to narrow the gaps among business partners. Accommodation for other cultures became one of the conditions for globalization theory that nations today adapt as members of the Global business community.

The conference was a moment that trade partners had the opportunity for the exchange of information about commodities. The events promoted the increasing role of diversity in international trade and immigration as a strategy, after the industrial revolution. The experience preceded the global Migration Renaissance after the world wars I and II.

The migration across globalization has increased the requirements for integration with peoples from various cultures for understanding integration. Countries with a high diversity population density as North America need a strategy model that those other continents may follow. The journey across the US and Canada for my graduate studies in international business became another study case that started from Minnesota, by the Amtrak Train reservation, connecting from Chicago to Washington, DC, to visit with the World Bank, USAID, United Nations Center in New York, and crossing in to Montreal, Canada to visit with the North American Free Agreement (NAFTA) Offices.

In Chicago, my first encounter was an Asian taxicab driver with a mustache, a common French origin word I had remembered about Paris, France, a man of long bear domiciled and known to the French by that name. I felt an international journey as a student in Chicago.

The Chicago visit included the international center in the skyscraper building overlooking the city and was met on arrival by a staff member. Later, I had a meeting with the director of the International Center, originally from Turkey. We joked about Turkey's inclusion in the European Union (EU), where the theory of globalization was invented and now linked to diversity and inclusion.

My next encounter was with the Mexican consulate and member of NAFTA in Chicago. I greeted the consular in Spanish, and later visited with the Italian consulate and spoke Italian I'd learned in Milan, Italy. After Mr. Obama became President, I already had his photograph that I traveled with to Canada during my research visit with NAFTA, as part of my international studies, and was asked about the election in the US at the time, and the possibility of Obama becoming the President. In reply, I said he was already a president! Being optimistic to my word on my return home, he became the forty-fourth President of the United States, a reinvention of diversity by electing the first black man, in my country I dearly loved, after centuries of the challenge for diversity inclusion as country of immigrants.

The next stop was in Washington DC, to visit the World Bank, where my credentials were inspected by a Ghanaian from West Africa for the visit, and later to IMF, and the United States Agency for International Development (USAID), on Pennsylvania Avenue. As I walk on Pennsylvania Avenue opposite the white house, I glanced in a store the artwork of Barack Obama on display as expected President of the United States, and being excited, as a stranger in Washington DC from Minnesota, I snapped a photo of the artwork.

In New York, I confirmed the testimony that the US is the World Marketplace, with most cultures represented. My next destination was across into neighboring Canada, in Montreal, a bilingual city of (French and English), with a diverse community environment across the border. At the border's stop for inspection on the popular Amtrak Train that commutes between the US and Canada, a male Canadian immigration frontier boarded the train first, followed by a female officer, who greeted passengers in French and English, a language I'm used to in Minnesota. On arrival in Montreal, Canada at night, communication with the public was in French at first, followed by most places visited. In the hotel that I checked in, it became Bilingual (French and English). At the counter was a Caucasian Canadian, followed by others including Asian, African Canadian, Jamaican, and a Brazilian medical Doctor. I realized that the world has changed, so are people and organizations at workplaces of various cultures, to remain competitive in the world marketplace. As I was in the hotel, I phoned my host contact with NAFTA Headquarters in Montréal, and his voice message response was in French. I felt mesmerized by the French language message, wishing it was a foreign language as the Italian I'd learned in Italy. As the voice message continues, an English version later follows. I felt Canada is a step ahead in diversity competence, and reflected on my sojourn in Europe with its Multilanguage system, but synchronized in a society ready for the multicultural inclusion environment. I soon realized that Canada was not just among the diverse countries but multilingual.

On the return journey to the US, the next encounter was an Attendant of the Amtrak Train. She was a US citizen that recognized my accent and said to me that her parents were missionaries in my country of origin in West Africa; she had lived as a child for several years. How you recognize the accent from that part of the world, I asked. She replied, "Because I grew up with that accent as an American," wow! A country that several thousands of Americans have lived and worked for over a century, after the returned of the freed slaves in 1822 to resettle in Africa, and founded Liberia, in West Africa. As a Liberian African American, I recognized globalization; diversity inclusion and accommodation are synonymous and will remain. The encounters show the need to harness diversity management practices and maintain the status in the world trade, by transforming institutional management competence for efficiency and productivity.

The US is one of the highest immigrants' countries on Earth. If so, how prepared is the system and Business institutions to manage in the 21st century and beyond? My brief story has clearly defined diversity from the perspective of people from various backgrounds. The book is unlimited to the leadership role to increase efficiency for productivity through diversity workforce.

INTRODUCTION

The changing conditions about workplaces and the role of Team Leadership for enhancing organizational performance transcend to globalization and demand for innovation in management and leadership to support organizational efficiency. Diversity workforce practices are under various codes, like Affirmative Action, Gender equality, Aging, and other categorization that demands a change to enhance organizational learning for improved performance.

The book discusses some specifics and roadmap for achieving diversity inclusion at Workplaces, as a priority to enable organizational productivity for efficiency. Leadership at organizational levels today is challenged by how to accomplish efficiency in a diverse workplace. The transcend to scientific organizational management after the industrial revolution has required societies with multinational cultural diversity to increase education in the workplace environment, including governmental and non-governmental institutions. Leadership deserves education for diversity workplaces to realize the mission and accomplish real-time equilibrium in managing, as Leaders are informed and educated about diversity workforce practices and its added value.

As a contribution to the discourse about diversity inclusion theory and the role of Team leadership in organizations as governmental, non-governmental, Universities, and corporations, this book provides cognitive knowledge of diversity workforce for Teams and education on cultural values connected to various cultures.

The content is useful for board members of corporations, governmental regulatory agencies, human capital management, and monitoring, including; workforce audit agencies, Affirmative Action offices, States, and federal agencies. All will find the book information useful for enhancing organizational responsibilities, to promote diversity inclusion under the Affirmative Action.

Team leadership represents the organization to enable productivity, and the ability of intercultural competence to overcome conscious and unconscious bias treatments. The book contains information and education for working Team leaders with no prior knowledge of intercultural competence in the multicultural workforce environment. It rekindles the need to value diversity inclusion etiquette and provide basic diversity Teamwork information, which can expose Team leaders in governmental and non-governmental organizations for managing diversity workforce. Though the book is not a course for diversity Team leadership (DTL), it provides some scholarly information about diversity Team management.

A diversity workforce Team leader can find the information and education for adjusting the leadership traits about intercultural competence, to lead Teams locally and globally with understanding. A lack of understanding of various cultures can undermine the organization's occupational health in mixed workforce management.

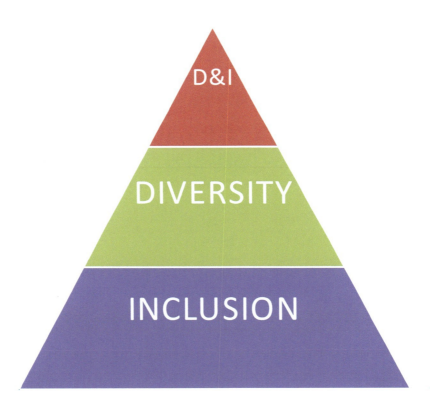

CHAPTER I

TABLE A: REPLICA OF EGYPTIAN PYRAMID BUILT BY DIVERSITY TEAM WORK 3500 B.C

©jfseekie@2019

TEAMWORK HISTORY, RESEARCH AND DEFINITION

The Diversity Teamwork history is traced to the adventure of the Nomads, construction of the Egyptian pyramid, the Washington D.C. monument construction, and the forming in the 1800s, of the Rockdale Weaver's cooperative of England to harness the potential for efficiency and productivity. Teamwork theory remains the symbolism of power among the workforce as it transcends modern management characterized by various practices, including transformational and transactional theories. Team practices are among the modern organizational management concepts. Unlike Teamwork of the past, diversity inclusion in modernity requirements for success demands a more integrated approach for achieving organizational efficiency and productivity.

PROPONENTS OF TEAMWORK

Before the emergence of scientific management, Team forming phenomenology was in Africa, where civilization emerged, including the theory about the Teammates formed to build the pyramid in Egypt. After the pyramid Teamwork theory workforce, proponents under scientific management include Kurt Lewin, a German American psychologist, John Fairhurst, Bruce Tuckman, Stewart Tubbs, Marshal Scott Poole, McGraths, Gersicks, Morgan, Whelan, Jensen, among others, who have advanced the theory of group dynamics, now challenged with diverse Team for a change in modern technology age Teamwork. The transformation of Team dynamics from one generation to the other has changed the perspective of Team culture. Diversity Team is an exemplary paradigm shift for diversity group dynamics. Max Weber, a German sociologist, is credited for his contribution to organizational management and the role of Teamwork. Other proponents of Teamwork among organizations included; Frederick Taylor›s scientific management approach, followed by Elton Mayo, who conducted the Hawthorne

Study, building bridges between Team and productivity in the organization. Others included Maslow and Carl Rogers among several.

As early as the 2000s, management Team leadership perception of customer service advanced to the accomplishment of management performance with greater customer satisfaction. The requirement of this gap remains the challenge in Global diversity organizational management systems (GDOMS), as a condition for supporting organizational productivity for efficiency. Teams in organizations were once thinking in the box (internal) when organizations were operating from an internal country model, now challenged by external Teams from other cultures. The ability to manage the workforce involves understanding diversity inclusion. Team accommodation in the organization is complex and demands intercultural leadership competence, which remains a hullabaloo among Federals, states, corporations, and NPO organizations globally. The culture and structure of organizational Teams have changed from 1800 to the 21st-century organizational management systems. Coping with the reality of intercultural competence has become a challenge for discussion among scholars. The consensus in styles of Team leadership will drive organizational productivity in the global context.

Diversity Management Team practices will yield to adaptation for the greater good of organizational development. A change in the organization can expect consequences as productivity and under-productivity for various reasons. The culture of diversity Teamwork in sports, community work, among corporations, the nonprofit industry, governmental, military, among others, and have the framework and direction about its accomplishment.

THE WAY TO ACCOMPLISHING TEAMWORK BEGINS WITH THE PLATFORM FOR TEAMWORK

Evolving realities about workplaces involve the role of Team leadership for enhancing inclusiveness, productivity, and efficiency as organizations transcend in globalization, including innovation in leadership traits for operational health and growth. Beyond Team formation, a monitoring system for check and balance to accomplish a Team leadership role can support the training of members to follow the mission for the accomplishment of the goal of the Team. An assessment for performance and alignment can also support organizational plan, as the success of an organization will depend on the successful working Teams for a diverse workforce environment, as discussed in proceeding chapters. Diversity Team leadership will respect employees' cultural values.

TABLE B: *DIVERSITY INTEGRATED DIVERSITY TEAM ANATOMY ROAD MAP*

©*jfseekie@2019*

POCAIE TEAM= PLANNING, ORGANIZING, COORDINATING, ADAPTING, IMPLEMENTING AND EVALUATING. DIVERSITY TEAM LEADERSHIP GROUNDED IN INTERCULTURAL COMPETENCE. HAVING DIVERSITY SUCCESSFUL TEAM IS AS HAVING A POKER TEAM IN CONTEXT OF GLOBAL MANAGEMENT.

FORMING AN INTEGRATED DIVERSITY WORKFORCE TEAM

Reinventing Team design and selection process of integrated team members from various cultures can enable innovation in managing diversity teamwork.

Diversity Team integrated Forming (DITF)

DIFT sets the foundation for the Team cultural shock absorbers, vertical or horizontal, how to resolve obvious conflicts and communication among members and overcome cultural barriers. Proper Team forming lays the foundation for a diverse workforce.

Diversity integrated Team Acclimating (DTIA)

DTIA is the pillar for Team member acclimation by motivation, through established procedures in achieving the vision, mission, and goals with objectives.

Also, reinforcing, coaching, and ensuring cultural barriers' correction as a capacity-building.

Diversity integrated harmonizing (DIH)

DIH will implement the Team's mission through monitoring and formative evaluation and corrective measures toward achieving the goals.

Diversity Team integrated Practicing and coaching (DTIPC)

DTIPC involves the sustainability of vision and mission by assessing diversity Team for success through continuing education. Because the diversity Team's structure and characteristics are demanding, it carries special requirements for success than traditional Team structure with members from the same culture.

Organizing diversity Team is conventional as reframed by theorists over the decades, including the modification by Tuckman on the theory for Team formation. Diversity Team requires cultural adaptation to adjust to working with Team members from various cultures over the short or long term. The difference in practices requires special emphasis to adjust to contemporary Team structure as advanced into the post-industrialism. The adjustment involves information and education for understanding to support inclusive Teamwork (Tuckman, 1965).

The challenge for diversity Team is unlike traditional Teamwork for cultural reasons. The traditional Team is centered on workflow cognition, while diversity Team balances cognition and alignment to overcome cultural barriers and enable efficiency for productivity in public and private services.

Diversity management Team (DMT) in this book refers to the middle management level involved with the diverse workforce management in the production, administration, and operation of an organization. It includes divisional managers, supervisors, and Team Leads. Team management extends to executive management responsible for designing and directing the policies affecting DMT that affect diversity workforce. Teams involving lower, middle, executive, and board management, have a leadership role in common, and the responsibility of organizational diversity management in globalization. Team management extends to executive management responsible for designing and directing the policies affecting DMT that affect diversity workforce.

WORKFORCE DIVERSITY TEAM LEADERSHIP DEFINED

Diversity workforce leadership in this book refers to the Team›s role in managing the diverse workforce, representing people in various cultures. Leadership competence for leading people from various cultures requires specialized skills as intercultural competence. Besides global cultures, the subculture from local affinities also requires special skills. The combination of various cultures has increased the responsibility of leadership information and education.

DIVERSITY WORKFORCE

The Office of Personnel Management(OPM) defines workforce diversity in two parts: "Diversity as a collection of individual attributes that together help agencies pursue organizational objectives effectively… a set of behaviors (culture) that encourages employees to feel valued for their unique qualities and experience a sense of belonging"(OPM.Gov, 2016).

DIVERSITY WORKFORCE TEAM

Diversity workforce is a Team composed of Team members with diverse cultural orientations. The three main divisions of diversity workforce are members from multiple countries, local ethnicities, and the members of the Team belonging to protected status as age, race, sexual orientation, gender, and disabilities for the US.

TABLE C: MAJOR DIVERSITY GROUPING GRID

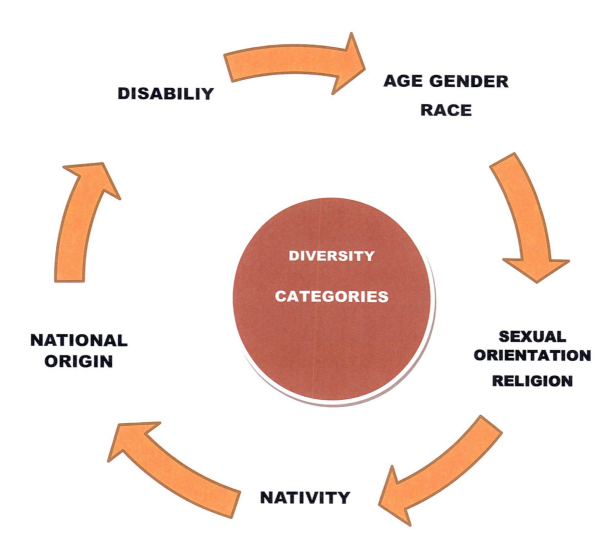

jfseekie©2019

WHAT IS INTERCULTURAL COMPETENT DIVERSITY WORKFORCE TEAM LEADERSHIP

The requirement of today's diverse world organizational authentic leadership role demands intercultural competence in leading a diverse workforce. Intercultural competence leadership role refers to the awareness of the worldview about other cultures and behaviors, and communication skills to interact across cultures. Intercultural competence involves attitude, learning about other cultural practices, and finding a way to communicate appropriately in a leadership role involving a diverse workforce. A leader may acquire intercultural competence knowledge and certification essential in leading organizations for the greater good of organizational leadership and development.

The ability of the Team leader will involve skills, knowledge, and dexterity to interact with various cultures. The leader will have experience in local and global diversity workforce inclusion and local laws. Additionally, Intercultural competent leader will have cultural intelligence, about; conscious bias and unconscious bias practices among the workforce, and the ability to distinguish between ethnocentrism and prejudice. A leader will have intercultural coaching skills required for managing conflicts among diverse Team members, with knowledge of multiculturalism and gender balance. The Team leader will lead Team members with cognitive skills and affection, using skills through effective intercultural communication and make the Team responsive to organizational policies to promote productivity. A diversity Team leadership will show a conscious and unconscious bias-free attitude. A competent intercultural Team leader will think cross-culturally and create an environment of Camaraderie by maintaining relations among Team members in promoting productivity. Leadership will recognize the intercultural values without compromising the principles of the organization's interest and uphold diversity inclusion by coaching members and discourage discrimination or bullying, among other exclusions. Understanding inclusion involves Affirmative Action and global diversity connected to workforce integration.

DIVERSITY TEAM LEADERSHIP ROLE

Diversity Team leadership role involves managing a workforce of multiple groups from various backgrounds and cultures, with the knowledge to interact with them through intercultural skills for achieving organizational goals. The role of leadership also includes managing the law supporting the affirmative action and the executive orders for enforcement.

ROADMAP TO DIVERSITY INCLUSION ENFOREMENT

The Diversity integration effort had been characterized by several laws, including executive enforcements by Executive orders number 13583, 2011, to promote diversity, Executive order number 13548, 2010, intended Veterans to accommodate citizens with physical impairment or disabilities, number 13518, 2009, harmonize and promote diversity inclusion across institutions nationwide, number 13171, 2000, promote Latinos in federal government employment, and number 13078, 1998, increase adults' skills among millions of Americans challenged by disabilities, and number 13564, in the year 2011, to address jobs and competitiveness (Federal Register, 2017).

SOME PRIOR ENFORCEMENT EXECUTIVE LAWS (D& I)

The EEO is supported by Federal and state employment laws enforced under the Equal Employment Opportunity Commission (EEOC), relying on the Affirmative Action law implementation at workplaces in the US. The laws protect people with physical impairment and veterans, among others, to adjust from the past to the present, including discrimination. Federal contractors, for example, adhere to executive order 11246, implemented under the Office of Federal Contract Compliance Programs.

TEAM FORMATION

Teams are formed in organizations with policies to keep them operationally successful. However, a Team model will align with the parent organization's goal, though Teams in organizations vary in activities, the goal of success is common. An internal or external Team will have the responsibility for accomplishing the vision, mission, and goals. Leading a Team involves a combination of leadership traits and value, as discussed in the later chapters.

CULTURE OF TEAMS (WEAK OR STRONG)

Team leadership literature discussed practices in Teams from various perspectives. The strength and weaknesses are common denominators of the Team. The similarity among Teams may show weakness or strength as characteristics to define a Team. Some common types of behavior among teammates include *LOW- FIVE GROUP, a* type of Team that requires constant supervision and may avoid added responsibilities and may contain the least critical thinkers.

HIGH FIVE GROUP

High Five Team members are those who think critically and perform beyond and may understand diversity workforce involving dissimilarities of Team members from other cultures, with experiences that can contribute to the quality of the Team's performance. They are critical thinkers, technical, and innovative. The *Alienated Team members* are submissive, self-managing, and critical thinkers. Diversity workforce can expect hidden facts about the cause of alienation feeling. For example, from a global diversity workforce perspective, underutilization of labor by lower-level jobs may occasionally occur in some cultures affecting Alienated Team members, and the challenge to human capital management.

The group needs research to increase the knowledge of the diverse workforce and support the efficiency and productivity of organizations. Conventional Team members are like the willing Trojan athletes, who may not win racing trophies but are motivated. Others include; hardnosed Team members (HTMs), with mastery (Daft & Marcic, 2006).

LEADERSHIP STYLE BETWEEN TRANSACTIONAL AND TRANSFORMATIONAL

The team in an organization needs a leadership style to drive it. After the introduction to Teamwork, several leadership styles had emerged, including transactional and transformational in recent decades, and adapted to management practices. Contemporary studies related to transformational and transactional leadership styles are the University of Texas, Michigan, and Ohio, focusing on organization.

TABLE D: ASSUMPTIONS OF THEORY X AND Y BY MCGREGOR

HYPOTHESIS VIEW	X TRANSACTIONAL TRANSACTION CENTERED	Y TRANSFORMATIONAL TEAMMATES CENTERED
HUMAN BEHAVIOR	PESSIMISM	POSITIVISM AND OPTIMISM
LOVE FOR WORK	DISLIKE TO WORK	REGARD WORK AS A NATURAL PHENOMENON
DIRECTION OF TEAM	AS RELIANCE ON SUPERVISOR	TEAMMATE ARE SELF CONTROL AND SELF DIRECTED/WHEN COMMITTED TO THE OBJECTIVES OF THE TEAM
RESPONSIBILITY	AVOIDS RESPONSIBILITY	ACCEPTS RESPONSIBILITY
CREATIVITY AND CHANGE	TEAM MEMBER LACKS CREATIVITY	TEAM MEMBERS ARE CREATIVE BY NATURE

jfseekie©2019

THEORY X AND Y BY MCGREGOR

McGregor's theory about globalization management appears suitable but demands a global theory for all cultures practicing management including high and Low context cultures as Confucian societies globally. Leadership and organization in high context cultures involve a Teammate and their assumption about independence, reliability, responsibility, loyalty, and interest (McGregor, 1966). Just as theory (X) and (Y) counteract each other's assumptions about Teammates and their practices, the reality transcends to diversity Team leadership. Team leadership for diversity workforce, therefore, is highly multidimensional, given the interaction required with the diverse workforce.

DIVERSITY TEAM A CASE STUDY EXPERIENCE

The production manager of the production organization realized that his supervisor's report was showing low numbers despite the increase in the number of production staff. Concern about the problem, the production manager of Asian background, decided to work alongside the production workers on the line and interacted with each member for a couple of sessions. The purpose was to understand the problem hampering the Team and the communication between Team members and the supervisor, and what was the problem. After speaking with several Team members of mixed cultures on the production line, the manager recognized the disconnection between the supervisor and the Team, and proved the ability about intercultural competence, through intercultural communication, and discovered the problem about intercultural communication gap between the supervisor, and the Diversity Team members of mixed cultures from Africa, Asia, South and North America, Caribbean, and the Pacific Islanders on the Team. Intercultural competence education is also self-directed learning (SDL).

COMMUNICATION

Communication between Teammates is relevant to understanding the job assignment details as it may require a repeat of the instruction to grasp the details. Ignoring the gap for understanding could cost the organization millions of dollars as it had occurred in many industries involving medical and nonmedical sectors. An organization wishing to avoid operational errors owing to communication needs to recognize the relevance of knowing and understanding among the Team in realizing efficiency and productivity. The Team Leader needs to promote the culture by getting the message among members. Communication among workforce members needs clarity. An example is the case study involving the intervention by the production manager. The study resulted in the determination of the intercultural communication barrier problem caused by the production supervisor working with a diverse workforce from various cultures. The goal of Team leadership for a diverse workforce is to realize efficiency through intercultural communication involving interaction. The Teammates' attitude toward work is a natural phenomenon of life as perceived under theory (x) and (y), and needs motivation as a tool for transformation, to overcome tendencies that can undermine the flow of communication among workplaces.

Communication between diverse workforces relies on understanding, which requires cognition. Cognition theory about knowing depends on multiple actions with the goal of understanding. Theorists identified three dimensions in research about cognition involving:

- ➢ Skill
- ➢ Decision
- ➢ Intelligence

A diverse Team leader will satisfy the requirement for leading a Team for the greater advantage of the organization, a problem usually ignored among some organizations. As errors occur in hospitals, like most workplaces, and the need for closing the gap must involve special emphasis on training for error prevention. Errors among workplaces in recent decades have provided evidence about the need for knowledge and understanding workflow processes among Teammates by increasing the learning of technology systems. Diversity workplace is a learning organization in achieving organizational output, and the high the awareness among employees, the better are chances for minimizing errors for efficiency and productivity. The Team leader will engage strategies to support members understand the workflow as the demand for understanding is among organizations for advancing quality diversity workforce and eliminating the fear of errors to promote productivity.

TRADITIONAL ORGANIZATIONAL HIERARCHY AND TEAM LEADERSHIP STRUCTURE

Traditional hierarchy is alert about organizational structures, involving all functions. The trail for managing follows traditional hierarchy involving a chain of command and communication through the direct channel for interaction with Team members. Team leadership requires personal and intercultural trait's competence interaction with a diverse workforce. The difference between the traditional hierarchy and intercultural Team structure indicates why an emphasis on Team leadership in modern organizational practices has claimed more attention. The total customer satisfaction (TCS) poses a greater challenge now than decades ago. Organizational development toward diversity inclusion is increasing total quality management (TQM). The responsibility for accommodating the increasing demand rests on transformation involving Team leadership traits. Team leadership has a direct link with the workforce to meet the challenge by organizational integration for the success of the leadership traits.

CHAPTER II

TABLE E: STRATEGIC PLANNING FOR DIVERSITY INCLUSION

©jfseekie@2019

THEORY OF PLANNING AND DEFINIION

The theory of planning recognizes the rational employment of the resources through established procedures for the greater good of society. The theory emphasizes setting goals by quantitative analysis of the environment and involves evaluation as an alternative solution to meet the demand and supply for the greater good of utility.

DEFINITION STRATEGIC PLANNING (SP)

Strategic planning (SP) is a systematic design of the future destiny for an organization through a schematic process. It involves setting goals for measurement and accountability to achieve it. The planning will include human capital and other resources, and the engagement of strengths and weaknesses. Other engagements will include stakeholders and their role in sustaining the mission, environment, and measurement of outcome, identification of customers to serve, and determining the quality of the product for the organization. Various models about planning are available, but an organization will base its strategic planning on change. SP is the approach by an organization to achieve the mission and shift the organization to another level, relying on human capital integration as one of the support methods. SP is an experience of the battlefield like the linear programming adopted for planning during the 1940s by the US Air force, as an innovative idea. The word "Strategic" was coined from the War Battlefield, and called in the Greek language, "strategos" referring to a General of the Army.

THE CONCEPT OF ALIGNED HUMAN CAPITAL STRATEGIC PLANNING (AHCSP)

Definition

AHCSP defined as a human capital plan alignment with the parent organization›s vision, mission, and goals with objectives. The vision and mission of AHCSP are separate from the parent organization›s plan. Conceptually, SP developed from planning theories based on three pillars; one, the need for organizational change (NFOC) from one stage to the other, supported by analytical data, circumstances, and resources to enable a change, (Two), identify the weaknesses to explore strengths and opportunities, (Three), evaluations from formative and summative stages of operation. The planning concepts can drive organizational change in human capital through established roadmap, scorecard, and collaboration involving stakeholders affected by the change. Beyond human capital are other stakeholders like customers to the organization, involved with the plan across agencies. For the US, the OPM as the human resources agency designed an alignment policy across the agencies for implementation. As an aligned human capital planning system, it is suitable for larger organizations as a federal system operating locally and globally. Organizations as governmental and Nongovernmental depending on location may have various characteristics of human capital diversity inclusion. D&I theories remain subjective phenomena and a reinvented practice in social science, as they involve social identities with similarities. A diverse group is composed of people with natural characteristics that define diversity realistically. Increasing constituents for diversity classification are categorized in two dimensions: (1) Group as gender ethnicity, race, sexual orientation, age, and those with mental conditions or disabilities, or others, and (2) belief system or language.

ENFORCEMENT AND ACCOMMODATION

Accommodation refers to place and convenience. To accommodate unconditionally provides a place for convenience to stay. An accommodation for integration includes workplaces free from discrimination as disproportionality in leadership participation ratio, which can have a ripple effect. Inclusion refers to unconditional admission without limit to some groups, from access to equal opportunities.

TABLE F: INCLUSION AND ACCOMMODATION

IN INCLUSION:	INTEGRATION:
CONDITIONAL LIMITED ACCESS TO OPPORTUNITIES	UNCONDITIONAL AMALGAMATION OF EXISTING COMMUNITY PREVIOUSLY DIVIDED CONDITIONAL: INCONVENIENT ACCOMMODATION
UNCONDITIONAL	UNCONDITIONAL CONVENIENCE: CONVENIENT ASSIMILATION ACCESS TO OPPORTUNITIES
UNLIMITED ACCESS TO: OPPORTUNITIES	

D&I   equation = Inclusion (I) = integration I = Acceptance

INTERNAL DIVERSITY INCLUSION AND
EXTERNAL DIVERSITY INCLUSION

A diversity inclusion based on citizenship will avoid discrimination. D&I are grouped into two views, including Global and Local Perspective. From the global point of view, it is a collection of people of mixed cultures from various countries, and the local perspective involves a collection of citizens with a unique set of cultures. The two views create an opportunity for a unified approach to defining diversity and reducing the threat of its acceptance, as advanced by the globalization theory. Globalization theory supports the systematic advancement of the connectedness of peoples, cultures, and the global marketplace for consumerism to prevail.

The globalization diversity workforce system involves the accommodation of belief system as Buddhism, Muslim, Judaism, and Hinduism; among others. The distinction between the two views about diversity classification involves the former, an assigned label of citizens in society for various reasons including; physical impairment as a disability or skin color, and sexual orientation. The latter is the natural self-determination of a belief system.

Under the diversity doctrine, there is no distinction among citizens because of disability, gender, old age, sexual orientation as LGTB, or other identities. The doctrine holds a view about diversity inclusion as citizens' agenda. An open dialogue supported by information, education, and organizational willpower like the OPM system in the US, could overcome the dilemma faced at workplaces about diversity inclusion. One effective way to address D&I conundrum is for agencies to use bureaucracy wisely to reduce the distance among employees, working in various locations and cultures, promote peer to peer interaction, and common language for interaction. The accountability system will include: adapting inclusion change culture, by coaching and promoting inclusive attitudes for results.

Division among Americans based on race is becoming reechoed among workplaces. Hiring practices are a challenge to the Affirmative Action Law and are in other cultures globally. To achieve adaptation requires rubrics, including education about acceptance and consciousness among the workforce.

D&I Justification

The problem of diversity inclusion requires continued observation and evaluation for more information and education among organizations. The mixed-method about diversity inclusion involve (1) Affirmative Action and (2) global diversity inclusion. Though diversity remains a controversial matter in literature, the need for increasing its value is supported. Research has indicated the challenges among cultures globally. Because of the challenges, meeting diversity equilibrium requires time and resilience supported by the public policy. Education about technology and other demand for workplace accommodation is necessary. Diversity inclusion will satisfy immigrants' and citizenship's criteria.

D&I situation in North America, including Canada and the US, remains changeable like other regions globally. In Canada, as an example, more than 5 million foreign-born is 17% of the mainstream population. The reality speaks to the consciousness for accepting diversity (CASSW, 2004). In the US, foreign-born are more than 11%, surpassing those of Canada and Australia combined. The combination of Canada, with more than thirteen percent minorities and the US with more than fifteen percent in the coming decades, could involve greater diversity inclusion, for the greater good for the accommodation of Minorities (AACU, 2002).

From the anthropological point of view, cultures will challenge inclusion based on Social Security. Therefore, diversity inclusion must recognize citizenship as a substratum for acceptance, and the distinction between an immigrant and a citizen needs to be respected. Organizational policies from the governmental and nongovernmental point of view will create policies to respect the value that diversity inclusion seeks to achieve and avoid manipulation.

FROM ETHICAL TO AUTHENTIC LEADERSHIP

The fortune 500 corporations and governmental organizations, in recent decades, had focused evaluation as a responsibility to manage effectively. Just as leadership is critical to the success of institutional management, the authenticity of leadership has evolved among corporate and non-corporate institutions to balance leadership deficit. The accommodation of stakeholders of mixed backgrounds in decision making will support the effort of the organization to balance policies. Authentic leadership touches organizational development locally and internationally. Contemporary gaps visible in some organizational practices include the nonprofit industry leadership deficit gap. Nonprofits include governmental and non-governmental institutions. Another example of leadership deficits among organizations includes Schools and universities in harnessing faculties, students, and administration. Also, authentic leadership trait was underrepresented by the action of the Olympic committee leadership traits by mismanaging children entrusted to the organization. The Hollywood narratives reflecting authentic leadership deficit was just a trumpet for sex abuse as one of the themes among organizations.

The perception of the female by authentic leadership occurs among institutions. The example includes the way they are treated by some leaders in some organizations.

The challenge of leadership deficit includes an authentic leadership trail as it continues to characterize organizational management. Organizations need to improve leadership practices through training for innovation, to overcome barriers to inclusion for efficiency. Leadership traits for leading diversity organizations need to comprehend diversity inclusion. The trend in leadership improvement claims the attention of other industries to reinvent the competence and reflect the aspiration of authentic leadership. SP tool used to design an operational policy can support organizational change management involving human capital, to achieve high performance, based on the leadership in charge.

The leadership deficit gap needs to be narrowed over the next decades, to mitigate the challenge as organizations become more complex to manage. Among the problems that have attributed to the downward trend in organizations is inadequate knowledge of diversity leadership. The gap hurts organizational efficiency as the responsibility rests on the leadership trail. An authentic intercultural competent leadership, for example, is open and inclusive of diverse stakeholders, based on is awareness principle, but not all organizations have prioritized a solution for efficient and productive services.

THE WAY TO STRATEGIC PLANNING ROADMAP

Diversity inclusion is a complex adventure among human resources management. Every society has some control over policies as a global practice. Among the global imperatives for governance includes reinforcement on a global scale. Every country has a labor law, and reconciling remains the challenge for universal standard human capital practices. The example is the treatment of labor in the Eastern and Western regions based on various reasons. A general roadmap, for internal and external organizational D&I engagement, will aim at generating interest, involving: adaptation agreement rate as an organizational change dynamic and the willpower among organizations can support its implementation.

As organizational leadership decides to overcome associated diversity inclusion barriers (ADIB), the plan may lag over the years owing to a lack of consensus among leadership. An unbalanced diversity inclusion practices can affect an organization and the economy by millions of dollars in losses caused by the workforce under motivation that may affect productivity and efficiency. Unlike an evaluation plan, the accomplishment of the goals of the D&I plan will involve labor Deskilling and Reskilling through open policy dialogue. The plan for inclusion by an organization will have characteristics about project management and a logic model with time-line, retention, a system of skills required, hiring, and HRD.

EVALUATION STRATEGIC PLANNING

A strategic planning board as a transitional Team manages the diversity inclusion. The board faces out, as the plan is achieved and integrated within the organization. A human capital strategic alignment system requires assurance of success at the end of the period, as the board retires. Diversity inclusion plan will involve more than human capital inclusion, to other opportunities among organizations. The goal of the plan is for the realization of diverse workforce integration over the life cycle of the organization. No quick fix for inclusion plans, and requires constant review for success. Diversity inclusion plan as coordinated under the auspices of the OPM federal wide scheme, involves human resources (HR) functions, to enforce implementation by agencies, and needs to recognize the historical barriers in overcoming those obstacles to inclusion. The barriers include intentional and unintentional action that undermines inclusion. An example of barrier includes unconscious, implicit, and conscious biases, some attributed to the abstinence of competent intercultural leadership among organizations up to the 21st century. The reason for the enforcement of the employment application process is for adherence to the US congressional authority Management Directive (MD715). The process is among the categories including:

- ➢ Demonstrated commitment from agency leadership
- ➢ Integration of EEO with the agency's strategic mission
- ➢ Management and program accountability
- ➢ prevention of unlawful discrimination
- ➢ Efficiency
- ➢ Responsiveness and legal compliance (www.eeoc.gov,2019)

ABOUT MD 715

> *"Management Directive 715 (MD-715) is the policy guidance which the Equal Employment Opportunity Commission (EEOC) provides to federal agencies for their use in establishing and maintaining effective programs of equal employment opportunity under Section 717 of Title VII of the Civil Rights Act of 1964 (Title VII), as amended, 42 U.S.C. § 2000e et seq., and Section 501 of the Rehabilitation Act of 1973, as amended by Pub. L. 99-506, 100 Stat. 1807, October 21, 1986" (www.eeoc.gov,2019)*

The MD715 requires agencies to engage a proactive role in the employment process, including identification of potential discrimination triggers from the application process to overcome any barriers. The directive further allows monitoring and eliminating barriers, and demands agencies to show that employment opportunities are free from discrimination.

Because MD715 attaches interest in eliminating the obstacles to effective diversity inclusion, agencies are obligated to prevent racial and other labels like national origin, sex, age, and physical impairment among affinities. A cross-sectional assessment by agencies supports the elimination of barriers involving performance evaluation and identified obstacles that can impede the achievement of the congressional mandate.

SELF ASSESSMENT

Barriers identified by self-assessment involving denial for equal employment opportunities as implicit and unconscious biases involve internal agency policies and includes; application processing, work performance evaluation, and promotions among organizations. Eliminating the tedious processes for evaluating and implementing barriers can minimize the processes by common sense to show that it is unambiguous.

For example, between groups of highly skilled affinity members in a department placed in clerical positions, while supervisors are with low skills without degrees are represented in a large number. The annual evaluation should justify the condition. Another easy approach is the annual departmental reporting should reflect each element of discrimination instead of combining all departments. As each department provides evidence of a barrier, it becomes easier to identify impediments to solving the problem as anticipated under MD715. The separation of females from the males in finding a solution to the problem of inclusion challenges the desired outcome. Another hidden agenda about the flaw is the internal reward of some employees to silence and stall inclusion. Employees should contribute through an open system of "suggestion box" without their names, to report a hidden problem without repercussions. Their input can contribute to solving the problem hampering MD715. In large organizations, the participation of employees in discussing issues confronting diversity inclusion can help identify the challenges. The Statistical identification of disparity will support solving the problems like the abstinence of affinity members in capacities as supervisors, division heads, managers, directors along the hierarchy chain. The rationale for assessment of barriers to diversity inclusion and the strategy for elimination will include occupation by affinity members proportionately at high levels (EEOC.Gov, 2019).

Why D&I

In recent years, diversity inclusion had been the concern as organizations reinvent systematic managerial change to allow accommodation. Diversity workforce hiring practices needs to be symmetrical with Affirmative Action law and MD715, as inclusion challenges cultures for adaptation. Administrations in recent decades had strived to advance inclusion, but the challenge remains among agencies and corporations for reinforcement. To overcome the dilemma, the OPM alignment model has begun to accomplish enforcement across agencies for the greater good consistent with ethical responsibility.

A disgruntled workforce with unbalanced diversity distribution, may become unproductive, and hurt the economy in several ways. The result can affect expected productivity owing to the lack of motivation. As recent as with Obama's administration, preceded by past administrations, the importance of real-time diversity inclusion remains a challenge. The question is why diversity inclusion solution is a slow-moving agenda, and the answer is to identify the weaknesses and adopt policies to overcome the status quo syndrome (SQS).

WELCOME DIVERSITY

An Organization can adapt D&I policy through corporate culture. A diverse workforce is fluid in today's organizational planning with tolerance for inclusion. The awareness among workforce leadership will uphold policies to enable accommodation, by maintaining core values about alertness, increasing organizational productivity, and welcoming diverse workforce by action from, leadership levels to lower ranks.

The evidence about diversity mix feelings among cultures is now recognizable, contrary to some viewpoints. The experience in other regions as the European Union is self-evident.

When former US Secretary of State, Madeleine Albright, commented on the state of the direction of globalization and its problems, I consent to her view, as it is becoming a reality that globalization is not without problems of immigration and integration. Therefore, overcoming the obstacles will have special consideration to defeat the general barriers to diversity in the global context. Diversity inclusion rejection has special consideration for enforcing a strategic plan. To overcome the barriers connected with practices at some workplaces caused by psychological reasons, including the reluctance by some recruiters to be transparent, organizations need a check and balance system with innovative guidance that can prove openness by verification. In contemporary diverse workforce hiring practices, eligibility as immigrant and citizenship is crucial for mixed citizens who must enjoy the benefits based on qualification to serve in professional practice, including leadership roles. The history of Affirmative Action over the decades involving hypocrisy still leaves more room for improvement.

D&I ORGANIZATIONAL CULTURE

'Diversity inclusion is principled on citizenship.'

Diversity inclusion values a mission based on principles of the diverse population and recognizes the relationship. D&I management requires the value to overcome common barriers among organizations. Theorists designed organizational management practices and recognized the need to identify the added value for achieving the organizational mission. As inclusion means more than just accommodation to globalization, it extends to integration and citizenship, which remains one of the arguments about diversity inclusion.

WHY DIVERSITY INCLUSION EVALUATION

Affirmative Action is a sensitive law, which has faced challenges to overcome barriers for implementation. The direct engagement of the stakeholders will reflect the opinions through the feedback to overcome judgmental conclusions as unconsciousness bias. Annual reports need to reflect the special emphasis section as independent input from the affinities to show the direct input from affinities in finding a solution to the problem of inclusion.

Special emphasis groups of employees as stakeholders among organizations can identify the barriers to accomplishment through the annual MD715 directive reports as an input. The input may include hypocrisy and other unknowns among the barriers. Independent feedback under the MD715 can contribute to overcoming the barriers. The feedback would provide information that Congress seeks to understand the problem hindering the effective implementation of the MD715 through public opinions. Dr. King's nonviolent theory supports openness for the voices of the victims of exclusion to be held. The black women pipeline strategy to evaluate women's disparity in federal employment is another example of a model approach gender balance, intended to achieve Equal Gender Affirmative Action (EGAA). Diversity inclusion evaluation will address the protected population unambiguously.

Among the steps to avoid ambiguity, the OPM as an example has introduced employees' annual survey, which received several thousand comments as evidence of the problems to be resolved through D&I. The problem of diversity inclusion transcended the scientific management era, and the emergence of globalization has reframed the dynamics for preventing discrimination. Diversity policy without education and accountability can undermine the corporate culture and contribute to under productivity. To build cultural intelligence involves practical observation skills for the understanding of the diverse workforce.

The evaluation of D&I can determine the level of inclusion of the protected population participation rate and their direct engagement at workplaces. Affirmative Action law has faced challenges to overcome barriers for implementation over the decades. The direct engagement of the stakeholders is to reflect their opinion through the feedback, and overcome judgmental errors, as unconsciousness bias barriers. Annual Affirmative Action reports need to reflect the special emphasis section as feedback from the population challenged by inclusion under the MD715. The feedback will show the direct input from the affinities in finding the lasting solution to the problem of inclusion.

The responsibility of the leader is to implement management policies. Organizational policies will guide the obstacles connected with the implementation of diversity workforce policy for the greater good. Managing diversity is a complex adventure, and the organization will embrace cultural differences and measure the acceptability rate of minorities. To realize the diversity inclusion goals involve two approaches among alternatives. They include: first, the management of the organization's plan and alignment of goals for the growth of employees. Second, the organization creates awareness, information, and education about cultural differences in the workplace. The policy for a diverse workforce will overcome barriers, and should not have a hidden agenda, but open to the employees.

AFFIRMATIVE ACTION AND DIVERSITY INCLUSION

The continue problems between Affirmative Action agencies and employers regarding effective diversity inclusion are evident in conflict cases. The problems about inclusion involve workforce and employers represented by corporations, state agencies, federal agencies, nonprofits, and international agencies. As observed from organizational internal diversity workforce management practices across organizations, reduction in tension about coping with the problems depends on leadership intercultural competence, in managing diverse workforce members from various cultures, and motivation for efficiency. Intercultural competence is an emerging theory about managing a diverse workforce. A diversity inclusion challenged by bureaucracy and hypocrisy can cost governmental and nongovernmental organizations enormous losses annually. The culture of Team leadership for middle management affects multiple responsibilities, which require high-level competence, including intercultural competence, and needs special attention among organizations to overcome underperformance that organizations seek to defeat.

From the organizational management point of view, the outcome should allow policies to accommodate diversity inclusion for the realization of operational efficiency and productivity through quality services.

CHAPTER III

TABLE G: CHAPTER THREE MAP

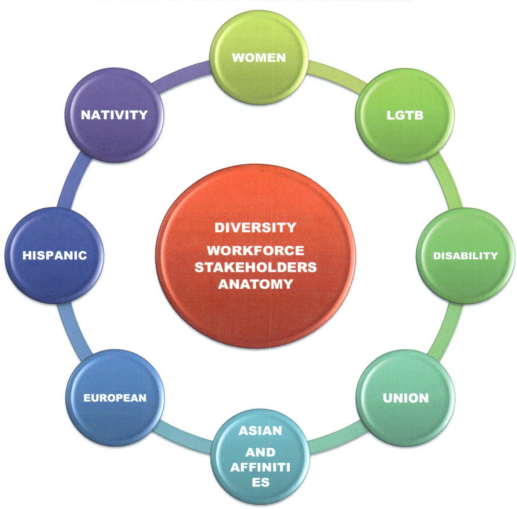

©jfseekie@2019

TEAM GROUP CONTACT THEORY

The contact theory was coined during the racial segregation in the US by Gordon Allport, in 1954. The theory discourages the gap created by the culture of segregation and encourages interaction among the population as an innovation. Interaction among the citizens is a diverse intercultural tool and opportunity for transformation to equality. The contract theory supports intercultural competence for interaction in harmony with the propensity to interact among Teamwork.

A theory is needed for today›s diverse workplace environment involving tension among diverse groups from internal and external cultures, working together for the common goal of organizations. Barriers as prejudices between groups can result in conflicts and need professional management practices. Overcoming conflicts can harness cooperation among groups. The roadmap to diversity Team management begins with the ability of the leadership to interact with a diverse workforce amicably, for a society divided by race and other verses.

HYPOCRISY

Hypocrisy by leadership can undermine motivation and productivity. Like intercultural competence leadership skill deficit, the workforce migration has challenged the balancing of internal and external cultures, and demands for the roadmap for accommodation with understanding.

Contract theory provides the evidence required for having a successful Teamwork. The theory is litmus testability of a diversity competence leadership. According to the theory, for groups to work in harmony, the level of understanding is tolerable, especially in the post-racial society characterized by racism, with the probability of hate and slurs. The reduction of tension among groups can promote workplace stability for productivity. Contact theory enforcement in federal, state, and corporate workplaces could save millions of dollars by reduced cases of conflicts among employees and management as the cultural affinities increase (Allport, 954).

The tensions and conflicts will exist among the workforce community of mixed groups of various cultures. Intercultural competence leadership for the public and private sectors can overcome the dilemma through intercultural theory, which advocates for a reduction in tension and conflicts among the workforce among organizations for a successful Teamwork interaction.

AFRO CENTRIC FACTOR

The stability among diverse workforce groups is essential for engagement. After Affirmative Action law, the protected population as the Afro-centric community remains challenged by a leadership role in some sectors in societies. The challenge for inclusion of the Afro-centric or minority community members in North America, EU, Australia, South Africa, among others is an example of the need for leadership intercultural competence to contribute to the Affirmative Action law and the global inclusion strategy, based on migration for integration.

SYMBOLISM OF INCLUSION

A weak internal inclusion policy can hurt organizations in several ways, when not properly monitored. The US and South Africa have demonstrated the symbolism of diverse identities with Nelson Mandela and Barack Obama as evidence of inclusion in mixed societies with a history of exclusion among the population. A symbolic gesture will flow from top to bottom and integrated based on the Postpositive paradigm, which values a positive reality in modernism.

Positive Teamwork can contribute to organizational productivity and efficiency. Management needs to make sure Teams remain bound to accomplish the same goal. Some organizations may overlook conflicts among Teams, which can undermine productivity with consequences on profits and losses.

STRATEGIC PLANNING REQUIRES RESOURCES SUPPORT

An organization wishing for an effective human capital inclusion plan will prioritize allocating resources for its successful outcome. The theory holds a view about the successful implementation of a plan based on the allocating resources for implementing the plan. The implementation of a plan in organizations with a watchdog agency as the congressional management directive (MD715), can contribute to an improvement for inclusion gaps, depending on the willpower of the leader at the top, who must have intercultural competence education, as contemporary leadership practices in globalization demands. The shift to organizational strategies can overcome the leadership deficit.

TABLE H: TRIANGLE STRUCTURAL BARRIER ANALYSIS

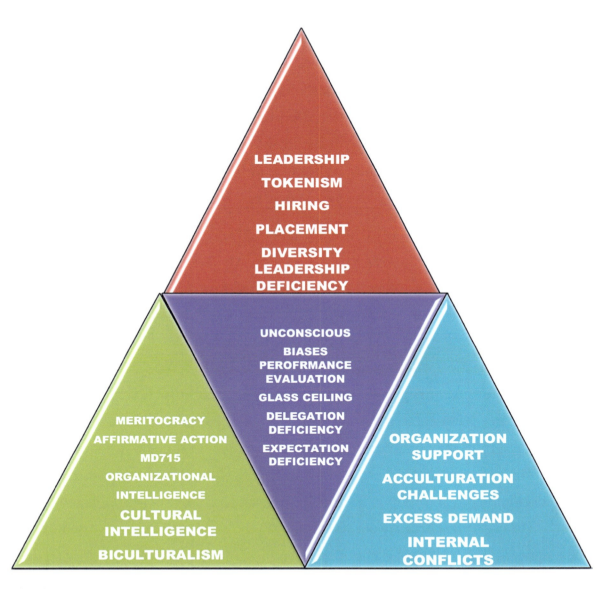

©jfseekie@2019

BARRIER ANALYSIS

Barrier analysis can identify the errors and encourage decisions for organizational change to enable inclusion. A plan, therefore, will need a powerful vision and a mission. An example is Dr. King's vision and "nonviolent" theory that remains thematic of the power in a vision and mission. To realize desired organizational human capital management success is to meet the goals through successful planning for minimizing barriers to organizational success. A plan for human capital can become flawed because of inadequate capacity among agencies to accomplish an alignment protocol, which can serve as a roadmap for coordinating policies to minimize errors and flaws.

RESISTANCE AND AFFIRMATIVE ACTION

Stakeholder analysis will show a strategic view of issues concern to them, like the policy involving Affirmative Action in a working environment, which can reduce tension during change management. The reason, the information will flow across the organization in a change management situation (CMS) to avoid resistance. Employees may resist change that affects them or indirectly, and overcoming resistance is critical to the implementation of a change. A hidden resistance may hurt the operational health of the organization in several ways, reason stakeholders' role in the change management plan is significant. Leadership may have no direct control over the resistance in a system used to a predominant ethnic group in leadership roles, and a change plan could face challenges at various levels. The organization can avoid surprises from the employees' reaction by educating them about their rights to know as they accept the policy.

HUMAN RESOURCE MANAGEMENT (HRM)

The role of the HRM in balancing human capital integration under a plan will rely on ethical responsibility for a policy involving multiple affinities complex as the OPM. An organization will engage in planning to overcome obstacles to advancing inclusion based on activity and location. In a governmental environment as Public Service, human capital planning may include several agencies requiring an alignment system as the case of the OPM, across agencies to streamline the policy for conformity to affirmative Action. Each agency may have its policy for interpreting alignment process by OPM design to avoid contestation. A diversity workforce inclusion involving policy alignment across agencies may require rigorous reinforcement like the case of OPM focused on the inclusion supported by the Affirmative Action Law. The plan for diversity workforce design will focus on local and international operating environments and legal jurisdiction. The private sector will learn from governmental agencies about the design for inclusion policies and practices, as human capital management challenges a model for the internal and external organizational solution to diversity inclusion, which has become a global challenge.

TABLE I: GLOBAL DIVERSITY WORKFORCE ALIGNMENT FRAMEWORK MODEL SAMPLE

©jfseekie@2019

LPD: LOW POWER DISTANCE CULTURE

HPD: HIGH POWER DISTANCE CULTURE

STAKEHOLDERS

The condition for the success of HCSP may depend on the stakeholders as employees among organizations as federal, state, nonprofit agencies, for equal rights and opportunities for inclusion. Increasing intercultural competent leadership involves vigorous education through dialogue with managers, leads, and supervisors to support the positive effort and enable principled diversity inclusion practices. As workforce members are informed about inclusion, they can view the effort and understanding to avoid rejection. The history of Affirmative Action has shown the need for overcoming lapses in diversity inclusion's implementation. Organizational transition affecting human capital involves changing to innovative ways. An authentic leadership style can determine procedural justice for change management. The stakeholder's role in organizational support will involve the participation of employees as evidence of the organizational culture of transparency. Organizational Planning in contemporary practices will include human capital with themes as diversity inclusion, Affirmative Action, and diversity workforce integration, which requires authentic leadership traits. The stakeholder's role in organizational support will involve the participation of employees as evidence of organizational culture and the leadership in charge. Planning in contemporary organizational development includes human capital, with themes as diversity inclusion, Affirmative Action, and diversity workforce integration, which requires authentic leadership traits. In the changing global organizational development, resources proper management can guide the leadership deficit faced by organizational development (OD).

TABLE J: NONPROFIT-GOVERNMENTAL SWOT STRUCTURE

STRENGTHS
TALENT BASED
EXCELLENT PUBLIC SERVICE
HIGHTECH COMUNICATION SYSTEM
LEARNING OPPORTUNITIES
TECHNOLOGY INNOVATION
GLOBALIZATION

WEAKNESSESS
ANUAL REPORTING ON TIME
REALTIME SERVICES TO AGENCIES SERVED
OVERCOMING LEGACY SYSTEMS
TRNSITIONNING
INADEQUATE HITECH WORKFORCE
SYSTEM IMPROVEMENT
EHTICS
DIVERSITY INCLUSION PLAN

SWOT

OPPORTUNITIES
HIGH VOLUME PROCESSING CENTERS
TECHNOLOGY CAPABILITY CLOUD
ANNUAL ENTERPRISE REPORTING
INCREASING SERVICES FOR COMMUNITIES AND AGENCIES
COMMUNITIES SCALE

THREATS
COMPETITIVE SERVCES ACCROSS AGENCIES
DEMAND FOR DIVERSITY INCLUSION
NEED FOR MORE TALENTS
ATTRITION
WORKOFRCE TECHNOLOGY GAP
TECHNOOGY ACCAMATION

©jfseekie@2019

STAKEHOLDERS' THEORY DEFINITION STAKEHOLDER ANALYSIS

A *stakeholder* is defined as a person or institution with interest in the resources of the organization or activity and has something to gain or lose whether condition changes or stays the same. *An analysis* is defined as a metric to identify stakeholders' level of interest or involvement, and how engagement can influence organizational success. The leader may alter how the organization will execute the necessary steps to limit stakeholder›s influence.

Who are the stakeholders in a human capital Planning process?

Stakeholders or employees are affinity groups affected by the diversity exclusion action and wish to overcome the challenge faced in realizing a successful outcome.

Aim of Stakeholder analysis
- ➢ Future of stakeholders
- ➢ Multiculturalism
- ➢ Relationship among the various stakeholders
- ➢ Priorities of concern

How we develop Stakeholder analysis
- ➢ Identifying with stakeholders affected
- ➢ Assessing the abilities of stakeholders to influence decision
- ➢ Identifying the potential for creativity

Why are stakeholders important

- ➢ help project planning
- ➢ Interest of all stakeholders /affected in the project
- ➢ help resolve potential conflicts or risks that could jeopardize the project
- ➢ Opportunities and relationship during implementation
- ➢ Groups can be encouraged to participate in various stages of the project
- ➢ Appropriate strategies and approaches for stakeholders engagement

How does the analysis interpret project

- ➢ Identifying the primary and other stakeholders interested in the project or policy concern.

How to engage stakeholders

- ➢ Dialogue
- ➢ Consultation
- ➢ Partnership in the project and their interest
- ➢ Working together
- ➢ Information gathering

TABLE K: STAKEHOLDERS ANATOMY

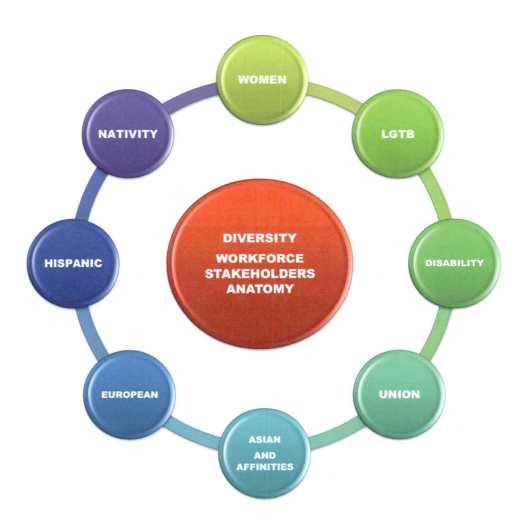

©jfseekie@2019

Human capital practices are idiosyncratic to traditionalist organizational management for governmental and non-governmental. Demand for inclusion globally will involve three angles: governmental systems involving cultures with Affirmative Action law, unitary systems as in Asia, EU or Africa, and Local and international nonprofit organizations (L&INGOs). The application of an inclusion model focused on human capital priority will align symmetrically for integration with the diverse workforce based on moral responsibility. An inclusion policy must meet the ethical requirement for the greater good in the interest of the organization. Global citizenship inclusion is a challenge to organizations, including states and federal governments, for policies to realize political, social, and economic integration with lesser resentments. The pressure to embrace an integrated inclusion is already costing millions of dollars and requires a model change in internal labor policies. Most agencies, including corporations, are challenged with balancing the diverse workforce and the need for thematic planning to overcome the challenges and avoid errors in the design of policies that could cause problems for the workplace environment.

TABLE L: STAKEHOLDER ANALYSIS

©jfseekie@2019

LP=low power, Hp=high powered

STRATEGIC PLANNING MODEL APPROACH

Strategic planning will involve a model that will align with the activity of the organization to realize an outcome based on the need. Several models provide a platform that an organization may use as a guide to align with activity. The six categories revealed in the literature include One, a conservative approach involving a plan not suitable for every organization, with a model focus on fixing the vision and mission of the organization. Two, a model for an organization with limited resources, but multiple problems with no clarity in vision and mission, but needs a redesign. Three, a model for organizational restructuring with changes over a period. Four, a model to allow organizational real-time change owing to environmental conditions. Five, a model for the alignment of subprograms in larger organizations with increasing technological adjustments. Six, a model for an inspirational approach based on high priority planning to drive the organization beyond the status quo with the participation of the board and stakeholders (Kaplan &Norton, 1992).

TABLE M: HUMAN CAPITAL STRATEGIC PLANNING MODEL SAMPLE FOR GOVERNMENTAL AND NONPROFIT

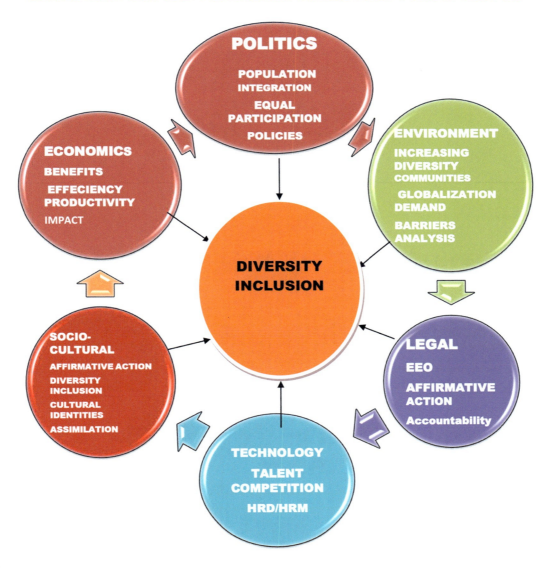

©jfseekie@2019

TABLE N: HUMAN CAPITAL WITH DIVERSITY INCLUSION IMPLEMENTATION STRATEGY MAP GLOBAL STRUCTURE SAMPLE

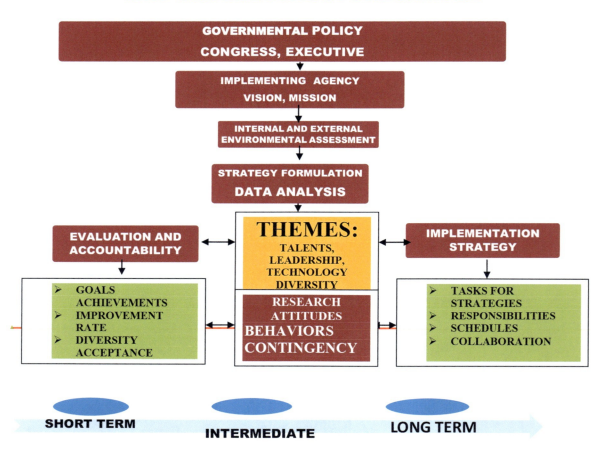

©jfseekie@2019

INTERNAL CONFLICTS

Conflicts among organizations are costly. For example, a management decision for a case involving legal judgment could cause the organization expenses for legal fees. Increasing organizational productivity supported by diversity inclusion can overcome operational deficiency and enable efficiency. Leadership among organizations will recognize how inclusion can improve the operational health of the organization. A balanced diversity workforce environment can maintain stability, among organizations, including public entities and corporations.

The cost of diversity inclusion for private and governmental organizations now ranges in millions of dollars in losses annually across organizations. In the application of inclusion policies, the process will predict a change in organizational structure that some employees may not be comfortable, and may need further education. Any design for inclusion will remain mindful of the pitfalls of imperfection in the model design for inclusion. An example is a situation of inclusion for leadership distribution as a dynamic shift. Another example is the distribution of power proportionately across the workforce ethnicities. The reality is that people as intelligent beings will demand their representation proportionally, and its absence can cause mixed feelings that threatens the security of an affirmative environment, with consequences. Remembering that one of the stabilizing agents for efficiency and productivity mix is the motivation of the workforce, as its absence is an apparition to the operational health of an organization.

AFROCENTRIC INTERCULTURAL HARMONY

The intercultural competent leadership relies on good communication and education as a strategy for leading diverse workforce groups by minimizing internal misunderstanding for productivity.

Leadership can engage in problem-solving methods to reduce issues like bullying and unconscious bias practices. Unfortunately, intercultural competence authentic leadership trait as one of the solutions to the evolving cultural Collision among societies remains indispensable.

The Mainstream Afro-centric (African Americans) workforce in the US maintains valued cultural identity as Diaspora afro-centric affinities. Understanding the Diaspora Afro-centric is important for group interaction by Team leadership as the case with mixed ethnicities. Afro-centric community population for the US as an example remains one of the major diversity groups with challenges for internal integration. A review of organizations indicates the need for an innovative way of managing diverse workforce integration through inclusion education for mixed heritage groups' interaction at workplaces for assimilation. Communication between groups like the Afro-centric enables building bonds for an integrated workplace community. As the generational transition unfolds, each subculture maintains identities and collective understanding of the melting pot to which workplace and living communities are synonymous with interaction and integration that inclusion seeks to overcome.

A SAMPLING OF HOW TO LEAD TEAM AMONG DIVERSITY WORKFORCE-COLLABORATION

Collaboration among diversity workplaces need the speed to explore the Anxiety uncertainty management theory (AUM), credited to William Gudykunst, to enable intercultural communication among social groups (Gudykunst, 2005). The theory, like the contact theory, supports communication efficiency and adjustment in reducing intercultural anxiety among multicultural societies, including diversity workplaces. The theory also connects to cultural variation among groups as the African American and Africans as an affinity and their communication involving virtual, technology, face to a face as social groups (Thomas, 2001).

Workplace collaboration will involve the communication and accommodation theory (CAT), credited to Howard Giles, and recognizes the interaction among social groups through communication theories for the transfer of messages among members from various cultures, which demands intercultural communication skills(Giles et al.,2010). CAT and AUM support the requirements thematic for building collaborative road map across cultures. Collaboration among teams needs intercultural communication skills as an instrument for interchange among members for collaboration synergy through openness and trust. The goal of the strategy is for the realization of integration over the life cycle of an organization. And, there is no quick result and requires constant review of the plan's implementation. In achieving quality management requires overcoming the status quo and shifting from the old order of predominance in leadership by majority ethnicity to include minority ethnicities proportionately in the postmodernism 21st century.

TEAM MASTERY IS A VISION AND AVOCATION

An organization also learns through learned Teammates found in the diverse workforce with highly skilled workers. Personal skill proficiency (PSP) enables learning through clarifying and expanding the knowledge and being more realistic to achieve a vision. In system learning, in creating a big picture requires support for Team mastery. The Team model involves unifying and increasing Teammates' ability to realize results, including; skills-building for a shared vision. Team members can do more and learn better as a group occasionally. Team member learns and grows by holding dialogue and engaging genuine thinking process. A mental model is a metaphor about how a Team sees itself by looking in the mirror to correct the errors for change and innovation. The difference between perception and the real-world, as explained by the model, reflects how the Team understands the organization through learning about the workplace (Johnson-Laird, 1983).

THE ROLE OF PROBLEM SOLVING SKILLS COMPETENCIES FOR

Problem-solving responsibility among Team leaders will include understanding a diverse workforce. The problem may arise from conflicts among diverse workforce involving intercultural, people dislike, and workflow hindrances. Finding a solution requires a schematic approach. Related competencies in finding solutions include collective judgment and comprehending skills. As a decisional tool, Problem-solving skill supports Team leadership in deciding on complex issues. The process for finding a solution may involve data collection to identify the problem before finding the solution. The understanding of the problem creates a comfort zone for engaging the solution. Conflicts will always be among Team members involving diverse workforce as cultural clashes, communication barriers, among other issues, will arise from time to time.

CHAPTER IV

TABLE O: WORLD MAP WITH POWER DISTANCE
LOW AND HIGH CONTEXT CULTURES

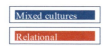

TWO MAJOR GROUPS SOCIAL SYSTEMS OF DIVERSITY WORKFORCE TEAM S -IN GLOBALIZATION CULTURAL DISTRIBUTION (HPD -LPD) BASED ON CULTURAL POWER DISTANCE

After Greet Hofstede coined the idea to measure cultural relationships, research today on global cultures, credits him for his work, as more studies continue to advance globalization. Diversity workforce cultural behaviors streamlining allows assimilation, depending on authentic leadership value for various cultures. The ominous task demands an interchange of information and education involving intercultural exchange that globalization seeks to mitigate and enable a uniformed diversity workforce. Alongside research on globalization social value systems, more research continues to bridge the cognitive gap among diverse Team members as employees and leaders in organizations.

TWO IMPORTANT DIVISIONS (LPD AND HPD)

Two important divisions of global cultural behaviors are the acceptable power distances of the population as a standard practice. They include High Powered Distance (HPD) and cultures that do not significantly accept power distancing known as the Low power distance (LPD). Power distance index (PDI) as a cultural dimension, allows special accommodation in a hierarchy system and respect for authority as reflected in a simple standing on the online system in LPD cultures. In opposite to HPD culture, social status in some society may place you at the top of the line at events as an acceptable accommodation and cultural etiquette to inequality. In the US, as an example, everyone stands online for services.

SITUATIONS RELATED TO HPD AND LPD SITUATION ONE

HPD allows people in society to accept inequality in power and culturally linked to Confucianism, a relational form of culture, which views power and relationship as synonymous and supports inequality, found in continental Asia, Africa, the Caribbean, and the Pacific cultures, among others. Teammates from these regions accept their superiors with more power, and employees may exemplify fear of autocratic bosses. Unlike HPD, situation two (LPD), leans toward the characteristics of individualism and values independence, recognizes power through self-responsibility for self-accountability as the case of the US.

IN HPD CULTURES -THE FOLLOWING MAY BE OBSERVED

The leaders in the HPD culture have more power and hardly questioned by followers, unlike leaders in the LPD culture, who can be questioned by their followers for justifying their decisions. Power distance index (PDI) as a cultural dimension, recognizes special accommodation in a hierarchy system and respect for authority as reflected in a simple standing on the online system in LPD cultures. In opposite to HPD culture, social status in some society may place you at the top of the line at events as an acceptable accommodation and cultural etiquette to inequality. In the US, as an example, everyone stands online for services.

A cultural dimension is the degree of inequality and equality between people in society and their norms and beliefs. In societies characterized by past and present discrimination problems, the unequal distribution of power and opportunities may need a guided law for monitoring, as we have in the United States.

LPD Team leaders may have a high level of anxiety and stress and are usually concern about security and procedure to follow as a yardstick, to check on the Team member. Because of the foreignness usually associated with the Team member from HPD, some LPD Team leaders may treat the HPD member with a level of mixed feeling. The several ways members from HPD can silhouette a leadership in LPD culture is through the uncertainty avoidance level, which measures the open-mindedness for uncertainty and ambiguity of Team members' experience.

The hierarchical system can always change depending on the circumstance. For hierarchies in a decentralized organization, some leaders can expect to have physical contact with their subordinates. The interdependence between the leader and the Team member in LPD happens when subordinates can consult about decision making. In contrast to LPD, the connection between the leader and team member in HPD can be based on relationships. For example, a son may replace a father in power.

The similarity among the two involves instances as nepotism in North America and the European diversity workforce. Nepotism, for example, occurs in LPD and HPD as a privilege determined by the leader and followers, sometimes based on ethnicity. To communicate in a diverse working environment, Team leaders from LPD will consider cultural differences and the predominating communication process in individualistic cultures.

The flow of communication from a low level, to a high level, is based on the bureaucracy. As the HPD and LPD Team members work together under an LPD system, several problems may occur in the exchange of information. They may include accent, perception, and differences in direction, quantity, and quality. For effective organizational performance, a Team leader from LPD needs to communicate with Team members through an intensive exchange of information on various issues to understand the situation of the workflow to enable performance. Ineffective communication and exchanges can undermine productivity and may cause performance problems because of misunderstanding. To understand several topics on modern organization needs effective communication among team members. In the US, as other diverse societies, most citizens have roots connected to various global cultures that Team leader needs awareness education or training for an organizational leadership that today's organizational specialization demands. Important characteristics connected with societies are relationalism and individualism as identities linked to the diverse population in globalization. An individualistic culture is based on an independent lifestyle and found among the Western hemisphere, while an interdependent lifestyle culture is found in Africa, Asia, and elsewhere.

OTHER CHARACTERISTICS EVOLVING

Other characteristics involve Feminism versus Masculinism syndrome, which challenges Male dominant role in society, involving job and civic occupations, and had been an acceptable global cultural relativist concept, now contested as a global agenda, supported by the theory of care. Uncertainty Avoidance (UCA), as a state of uncertainty about the unknown and the truth, is the hope for exploration for pragmatism and living with tolerance for the state of uncertainty. The gap involving gender and other values continues to receive attention by the increasing intervention by the faith-based institution, the value of family life in society, and the challenge to realities of life, as most societies are engaging innovation to realize the greater change, followed by other dimensions as speculation about imagining new things.

TEAM LEADERSHIP- WORKING AMONG VARIOUS CULTURES SOME ETIQUETTE NEEDED FOR DIVERSITY CULTURAL ENVIRONMENT (DCE)

An uncomfortable diverse working environment can impair Team and organizational efficiency in several ways, and avoiding it can contribute to Teamwork success. In creating a comfort zone for diversity workforce, some organizations are moving beyond testing diversity waters by engaging change systems, including a structure in Team leadership to deliver efficient services. Diversity workforce is challenged with masculinity and other gender equalities, as female ascend to top jobs in leadership, under diversity affinities continue to increase.

Building DCE is a daunting task for Team and organizational leadership. An organization can realize the goals for the delivery of services in the governmental or non-governmental organization and utilize DCE as one of the tools for achieving the desired outcome. The complexity of the problems presented by the diversity workforce described above requires finding a solution through competent leadership. Undermining the solution by presenting an image of a truce is a deception. Diversity Teammates are comfortable in a working environment to be productive and realize a level of productivity an organization wishes to accomplish.

SOME FACTS ABOUT INTERCULTURAL COMPETENCE

The phenomenon of intercultural competence is an evolving knowledge of leadership practices. Intercultural competence is a continually organizational learning phenomenology. Leadership training is relevant to certification, given its complexity involving multiple cultures. Some organizations are engaged in short workshops to prequalify Team leads, supervisors, and Directors to assume an intercultural competence. Because of the intensity of the learning required, organizations will make sure of regular updates for intercultural competence understanding. Multicultural integration with globalization has no quick fixes, but a strategic approach.

DIVERSITY CULTURAL INTELLIGENCE

The terminologies for cultural intelligence (CQ) and diversity workforce intelligence are an understanding of cultural values for workforce inclusion. CQ involves the inter-cultural competent skills for recognizing cross-cultural affinities for achieving inclusion. The strategy for achieving CQ can depend on the expertise about intercultural values, which may include the internal population, and those from other cultures, and the awareness of etiquette for integration with groups through cross-cultural communication competence (CCC). The topic of cultural intelligence and authentic leadership traits are obvious wordings that encapsulate attention in the literature. An intercultural study includes the cultural distance theory invented by Hofstede on global cultures and the emerging new terminology of D& I. The diversity plans for corporations, governmental, and non-governmental organizations for engaging inclusion can depend on Cross-cultural leadership effectiveness and cultural intelligence to defeat inclusion problems in most organizations. Knowledge, skills, and attitudes are evidence and reality about the intercultural competence organizational learning process. Because intercultural competence involves continuous learning, it beholds the organization to uphold the process of continuous training for organizational change.

Intercultural intelligence leadership effectiveness remains a challenge and needs research to support various questions regarding its effectiveness. For example, the nonprofit industry has a leadership deficit and needs several thousand managers projected to meet the global leadership demand for governmental and other nongovernmental organizations' internal and external operations, challenged by intercultural leadership competence deficit (Jensen, 2006).

The problems of a diverse cultural environment have now become an agenda for several boardrooms, as some authorities remain mindful of the hypocrisy about inclusion phenomena and the effect it can have on the operational health of an organization. An example is the case of the production manager in the case study. Some leaders may not be willing to admit the ineptitude to overcome the challenges faced by the diversity workforce Teams, including inadequate education about diverse workforce and the repercussion it has on the organizational output involving operational excellence, employees' motivation, quality customer service, and the effect on profit and loss in millions of dollars annually if computed. The need, therefore, for intercultural competent authentic leadership, is emphasized as an innovation in organizational leadership practices. Organizations need to acknowledge the changing workplace environment, involving the production and non-production industries, public and private services as governmental and nongovernmental previously ignored, and affinities as part of the melting pot. The effort requires an integrated organizational leadership role, involving intercultural competence. The need for internal operational change in systems now rests on how well organizations, adopt intercultural competence through Team leadership.

SOME CHARACTERISTICS OF DIVERSITY WORKPLACE CULTURAL ENVIRONMENT (DWCE)

In a dominant culture involving minorities as in the US, Europe, Canada, including multicultural groups, Team leadership integration can become challenging for groups as the hybrid afro-centric comprising mainstream and the emerging groups from abroad. The example of hybrid afro-centric community is the mainstream Africans of the US, and multiple other groups as (Ancestral Africans, Caribbean, Pacific, or blacks), under assimilation.

The ethnic domination in a leadership role in the regions is partly attributed to a high population ratio, contrary to the generality view from the lens of race, as an obvious phenomenon. While the unequal distribution of organizational control power is relevant to the determination of the Leadership integration within the workforce, assessment requires intercultural integrated skills.

➢ Value for diversity workforce cultures
➢ Delineation of gender equality and multiculturalism

In building DCE among cultural mix challenges, an intercultural dynamic approach for understanding to avoid a cultural clash, a diverse workforce will feel integrated than excluded, depending on the style of Team leadership. The Team leadership perspective on organizational policy view of inclusion can guide a working diversity workforce for achieving social and cultural equilibrium. In some societies characterized by individualism, power distance matters, and filling the gap is relevant to inclusion reinforcement. Reinforcement will involve adaptability for reducing cultural cubicle walls in the organization.

The Cultural Cubicle Walls (CCW) in individualistic cultures may hinder real-time services an organization may seek to achieve. And tearing the walls down can appear more difficult like the Berlin Wall. A diverse workforce for achieving flexibility in the work-flow for efficiency may require office cubicle walls without boundaries, to allow the free flow of work assignments and information among Teammates. The goal is to enable openness for the good of efficiency. During a job assignment conference of a group of new diverse workforce employees, the Team leader was limited by inter-cultural competent knowledge to interact with the group effectively. It became difficult for the new chief of the Team to express and communicate with members separated by cubicles for several months, costing the organization countless waste of hours, and a hindrance to efficiency and productivity.

CHAPTER V

TABL P: DIVERSITY INCLUSION ANATOMY

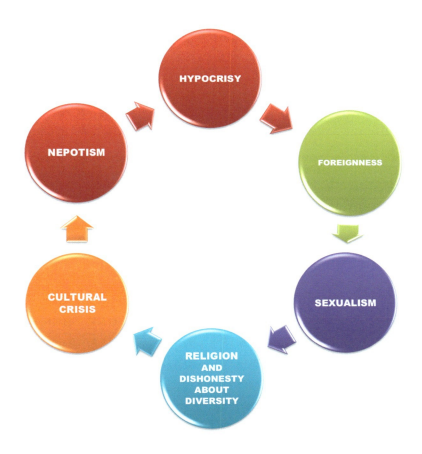

©jfseekie@2019

UNCONSCIOUS BIAS THEORY

Unconscious bias is unlimited to race and ethnicity and extends to various levels, including workplace promotion, hiring, appraisal, and assignment at some workplaces. Biases that occur at various organizations, like the case of the Cafe shop action against a Blackman, need the attention for engaging the responsibility required of consciousness and education about diversity inclusion. An ethical leadership decision can support a healthier workplace environment.

THE ROLE OF MIDDLE ACTORS IN D & I

Transunconsciousness syndrome (TUS) is a status quo behavior barrier to diversity inclusion by lip service for reducing and ending discrimination and is traced by the internalized systemic practices among individuals in organizations. It may occur under a system involving personnel evaluation, red tips in hiring and promoting at workplaces, and difficult to trace evidence of inclusion barrier, unless by a meta-analytic audit. For the reduction of barriers connected to an inclusion among organizations, intercultural competence leadership traits, and openness for the accommodation of opportunities at workplaces will need reinforcement.

SUPERVISORS

The method of deception for diversity inclusion mediocrity involves leadership roles. Team leadership practices in some organizations may have no formal intercultural leadership education, other than workshop training, but assume a first-line supervisory leadership role for human capital management, a practice common among large private and public service organizations. The first-line supervisors are leaders directly in contact with the employees for D&I accommodation and need intercultural competence to lead a diverse workforce for efficiency. The role of first-line supervisors as subordinate (leadership) can become mind-boggling because of evidence of education about intercultural competence for leading mixed culture workplaces among modern organizations. Intercultural leadership knowledge gap dyad for top leadership and subordinates are independent variables for D&I among organizations. Academics and some organizations advocate for authentic intercultural competent leadership CEOs, for managing and leading complex governmental and nongovernmental organizations, in the contemporary world.

The rationale is to balance the current gap of leadership deficit that challenges the organizational ethical responsibilities involving human capital management for organizational productivity and efficiency in globalization. Unconscious bias occurs at most workplaces in countries where affinities and migration have become the theme for assimilation. The reality regarding workplace security needs attention as we seek a healthier working environment. The insecurity of employees against workplace problems can causes work-related depression, resulting in the health conditions for employees. The diversity workforce problem is part of the causes of workplace depression disease to the awareness of the UN system.

The example of the workplace effect includes a story about a woman working in Public Service challenged by issues confronting her, which resulted in her depression, and suddenly died before submitting her letter of complaint. Neither employers nor the Unions can adequately guide against the multiple problems unfolding at workplaces for several reasons and the need for research to determine the future. The experience of workplace stress, as revealed in the European Union, involving billions of dollars in cost is self-evident of the need for future engagement of innovative ways to guide the diverse workforce.

DEFINITION IMPLICIT AND UNCONSCIOUS BIAS

Unconscious bias is a form of discrimination and wrongful judgments of a person based on a stereotype. It may occur unaware of the person committing the act. An example is a perception toward African Americans, or black people sometimes, being one of the outstanding barriers to overcoming discrimination for equal opportunities. Unconscious bias can result from bias judgment through stereotyping a person based on gender, age, race, physical abilities, religion, sexual orientation, weight, and national origin. Implicit bias is an attitude of stereotyping, which can affect understanding, action, and deciding unconsciously about a person. In diversity workforce environment, with a history of discrimination, unconscious bias is internalized among select groups, including leadership realms that may use it to favor or disfavor a minority member. The Affirmative Action law is not without criticism. A leader among mixed ethnicities may not favor diversity workforce minority members and could use a strategy through annual performance evaluation to shield against any evidence of unconsciously biased intent during procedural for a promotion. Imagine working with inadequate minorities in high positions as in governmental or nongovernmental, without the utmost power as described under the stakeholders' analysis of power distribution, to promote, demote, and dismiss an employee. When affinities are underrepresented in power structure of an organization, the gap for power may become disproportional, with consequences as in balance in leadership. The gap in power for minorities can invoke inadequate authority to uplift minorities' population in the workforce environment. A diversity inclusion strategy is about broadening the integration of opportunities, as meritocracy to prevent the unknowns, which can occur during the implementation at workplaces.

ROLE OF AFFINITY APPOINTEES

The distribution of organizational powers through the appointment of an affinity member in a higher leadership role in organizations under the Affirmative Action obligates the appointee to advocate on ethical principles for the protected population. The representation by the affinities to balance the power dynamics in organizations is for neutralizing and avoiding barriers to diversity inclusion. The action is to support the reduction in disparity gap and protect members from conditions that prompted the Affirmative Action laws and the subsequent reinforcement by congressional mandate (MD 715).

Among the Affirmative Action is the feeling about the role of appointees in a leadership role for vouching for adherence to the Affirmative Action law, as some appointees may feel challenged. Intercultural competent authentic leadership is invoked in organizational leadership practices as a reinvention of leadership traits, to encourage a new model of leadership. It can introduce the leadership role that focuses on diversity inclusion of Affinity Protected Population and beyond.

Literature needs to introduce models of intercultural competent leadership etiquette for leaders with adequate intercultural competence in the limelight of finding a solution to the continuous stall in diversity inclusion. After Dr. King's ultimate sacrifice, Affirmative Action law continues as a forum for diversity theory under the Eurocentric literature. However, inclusion remains without a theory as a phenomenological paradigm as literature continues to identify more. The African American affinities representing the mixed black race community, for example, is challenged by the role in leadership owing to the cross-cultural distribution characterized by low context cultural behavior discussed earlier. A diversity workforce inclusion involving policy alignment across agencies may require rigorous reinforcement like the case of

OPM focused on the inclusion supported by the Affirmative Action Law. The common native language across that community provides an opportunity for cross-cultural interaction by high chances than the African American Affinities challenged by mixed cultures, including language and communication differential. While this may need research, I leave it as an open debate hypothesis.

As representatives of the black communities in power politics, Obama and Mandela's ascendance to the offices of the presidency respectively signified the first statistical independent variables, for a diversity inclusion hypothesis of the past apartheid and discrimination regions. The legacy of the two leaders is a paradigm for other leadership jobs as Directors or CEOs, from the affinity communities to replicate. When former President Obama said that he was president for all in his country, some mixed feelings became apparent given the reconciliation that Affirmative Action promised for the victims of exclusion in his country.

In fulfillment of that promise, though, President Obama is a member of the African American community but was not the president for any ethnic group, and strived for implementing policies, which challenged the disparity rate that African Americans and Latino Americans are leading in national statistics by population size. The efforts included health care insurance, which has become politically challenged and a dependent variable for reducing those who cannot afford healthcare insurance, and in poverty. An example of inclusion at the top was Mr. Obama and Mr. Mandela, in the respective capacities as presidents are symbolism to be imitated by affinity members ascending to power. Affinity members may not represent quota but, must advocate for a policy for eliminating barriers to inclusion for all. The experiences of diversity inclusion as in South Africa, Asia, EU, Australia, North America, and elsewhere leave a journey to achieve equilibrium and remain a challenge to overcome.

UNIONS

Even in the EU, the home of the Polish Solidarity labor union leader, founded in the 1980s, and defended the cause of the workforce environment, but now affected by several billion dollars in the cost of depression among the European workforce, resulting from workplace environment according to studies. Workforce Unions, therefore, are expected to neutralize the issues causing tensions among the workplaces involving employees and employers connected to labor fair practices. Ethical leadership will make the workplace balanced by avoiding conflicts among Teams.

The workforce needs a reframed and improved employee Union system to address issues causing the increasing workforce environmental conditions connected to anxiety, worries, nepotism, and social exclusion, etc. For example, the diverse workforce in North America and the EU with challenges of migration and integration.

The Labor union system is not adequately engaged in a diversity of workforce accommodation in high migration regions like North America, Europe, and Asia due to the social and political conditions, and the inter-cultural education about emerging population, and still leaned on post-industrial revolution theories founded on the philosophies of transactional leadership.

A reinvented Union system would balance the current workforce tension and provide services needed to reduce the increasing pressure now leading the workforce to more depression caused by psychosocial hazards like mental health and worries. The industrial revolution institutions transcended to post-modernism, and need theories to protect the emerging diversity workforce in globalization, against characteristics reflective of the industrial revolution Labor Unions are focused more on work than employees. Globalization and the challenges for competition among industries remain the source of workforce pressure for change. Labor institutional agents like the labor Unions have inadequate attention on incidents affecting the workforce collectively. An example of the stress that affects the health of employees involves a cost of billions of dollars across organizations.

The experiences of stress, at workplaces, are evidence of workplace problems, including administrative and procedural justice. The leadership of organizations can calm the pressure on the workforce by reducing stress on employees, and contributing to a motivated workplace environment through leadership intercultural competence. Administrative justice needs close monitoring of the problems among Team leaders and employees. In cases like the release of information about an employee's records externally, which may impact an employee from seeking another employment remains a problem of privacy compromise, which needs review for policy guidance among organizations.

Administrative actions against employees need careful review for being free of prejudice and unconscious biases, as a social justice approach. The regular board needs to monitor the high turnover of the workforce for judicious management of cases involving employees' separation, to understand the reason citizens are leaving jobs voluntarily or involuntarily. Why are shootings at workplaces? Where is the intercultural competent authentic leadership? The situation of some workplaces countrywide needs assessment for various cultures that cannot be ignored.

WHO CARES?

The tension about conflicts at some workplaces is common. What is causing a threat among organizations? What is the role of Team leaders in maintaining stability by unbiased treatment of employees? The questions need answers. The board of directors for an organization expects a balanced operational health and quality output in keeping with business operational decorum. A management study can indicate that employees are under no excessive stress caused by the workplace environment.

The study strategy will support the operational health of the organization. The intent is to understand how the well being of the workforce environment and how employees› health conditions can influence and contribute to efficiency and productivity. The example of the problems of stress at workplaces is the European Union (EU) involving a cost in billions of dollars. The contemporary UN studies on workplace stress are a testimonial to the need for a balanced workforce environment (BWE), for the greater good.

The need for legislative advocacy, to address the threat faced by the workforce environment, is worth discussing, as studies have confirmed the need for intervention to mitigate the pressure faced by the workforce environment. An unhealthy working environment threatens capitalism in several ways. For example, human capital management with happy employees reduces the cost of health care, improved productivity, and reduced legal costs and increased profit and quality Public Services.

Among the biases of unconsciousness are ***National origin biases***, connected to diversity workforce involving people from other cultures and countries, and ethnic orientation bias based on affinity affiliation. Gender bias is the subconscious judgment in the selection of women over men during hiring process. ***Cloven hoof impression or collective guilt influence*** syndrome occurs when we generalize a single negative act to characterize a record for an employee and their job evaluation. ***Affirmation bias*** occurs when views are from influential people in the organization, even if such views are contentious, but used to justify an administrative judgment against and in favor of an employee. ***Corona effect***, when we evaluate an employee for praises at the boss, to justify his elevation to a high post among the diverse workforce. An example of the corona effect is giving kudos and highest performance ratings based on favoritism.

TABLE Q: SOME TACTICS THAT CAN INFLUENCE TEAM LEADERSHIP WITH DIVERSITY WORKFORCE

USE RATIONAL PERSUASION	FACTS,DATA,LOGICAL ARGUMENTS
RELY ON RULE OF RECIPROCITY	CULTURAL VALUES
MAKE PEOPLE LIKE YOU	HAVING SOMETHING THAT OTHERS VALUE (DEPENDENCY)
DEVELOP ALLIES	TALK TO FOLLOWERS
ASK FOR WHAT YOU WANT	DIRECT APPEAL INFLUENCE REMEMBER THE PRINCIPLE OF SCARCITY: PEOPLE ALWAYS WANT MORE EXTEND FORMAL AUTHORITY WITH EXPERTISE
CREDIBILITY	INSPIRE TRUST AND HONESTY

©jfseekie@2019

D&I equation = Inclusion (I) = integration I = Acceptance

©jfseekie@2019

TABLE R: MYTHOLOGY AFFIRMATIVE ACTION VERSUS DIVERSITY INCLUSION

©jfseekie@2019

TABLE S: AFFIRMATIVE ACTION AND DIVERSITY INCLUSION GRID

EXAMPLES OF AFFIRMATIVE ACTION:	DIVERSITY INCLUSION (D&I)

• Promote equal employment opportunity and to identify and eliminate discriminatory practices and policies (29 CFR 1614.102).
• Select, promote, and reward qualified employees, regardless of race, color, national origin, sex, religion, age, mental or physical disabilities, political beliefs, sexual orientation, or marital or family status.
• Eliminate barriers that impede open competition in the workplace, preventing individuals from realizing their full potential.
http://www.ars.usda.gov/aboutus/docs.htm?docid=1327
Employment Equal Opportunity office(EEOC)
Makes supportive regulation enforceable by the EEOC Employment Equal Opportunity Commission with states as counterparts. (www.EEOC.2017)
Affirmative action plans (AAPs) Provides prescription for a type of standards employers set from recruitment involving gender equality beyond what was once male and female dyad to multiple minorities, fulfilling social obligation such as LGTB disable, Veterans, and discrimination not totally absent locally and globally. With specific responsibility to increase minorities' presence in diversity workforce nationally reinforced by Executive order 11246 to ensure it extends to federal contract compliance.
	(EXECUTIVE ORDER)
	A new law committing to o understanding and accepting, recognizing, respecting, and learning from individual similarities and differences.
	    Executive order 13583, introduced to coordinate and promote Diversity through the office of Personnel Management OPM, which defines workforce diversity in two part: (1) "Diversity" as a collection of individual attributes that together help agencies pursue organizational objectives efficiently and effectively" (part (2) defines "Inclusion" as a set of behaviors (culture) that encourages employees to feel valued for their unique qualities and experience a sense of belonging" (OPM.Gov,2016)
	    The Executive order calls for intercultural competencies by leadership comprehending cultural elements as: political belief, religion, mental or physical disabilities, sexual orientation ,marital or family status race, color, age, national origin, sexual orientation, military ,or veterans language, status, lifestyle.
	    Enabling condition: relation to work value a diverse free of intimidation from freedom to thinking absence of stereotyping create an atmosphere for openness to learning from diverse community of workforce though openness.
	Prior executive orders:
	13548, 2010, increasing federal employment of individuals with disabilities
	13518, 2009 Veterans employment in federal government13171, 2000, Latinos in federal government 13078, 1998 increasing employment of adults with disabilities tapping skills of the millions of Americans living with disabilities (OPM.Gov,2016)

PERFORMANCE REINFORCEMENT FOR QUALITY OUTPUT/ SOME CHARACTERISTICS TO INFLUENCE

TEAM LEADERSHIP FOR DIVERSITY WORKFORCE:

- ➢ Exceptional skills about activity of the Team
- ➢ Situational leadership familiarity
- ➢ Coaching
- ➢ Charismatic
- ➢ Communication
- ➢ Intercultural familiarity
- ➢ Motivational
- ➢ Problemsolving skills
- ➢ Clarity in task direction

The 21st-century organizational development trend has embraced diversity inclusion for global organizational management practices. The internal and external workforce has changed, and diversity has extended to nations and the international business world. Demand for Team leadership with intercultural competence has become necessary to lead workforce Teams. A-Team leader needs an understanding of the communication dynamics to increase efficiency horizontally across Team members with clarity. Team learning extends in governmental, non-governmental organizations, and corporations to think insightfully and innovatively. The analogy reflects the need for closing the gaps among diverse workforce environment. Team mastery strategy will invoke the learning of new things and adapt to organizational development among diverse workforce management practices.

ENABLING DIVERSITY IN THE WORKPLACE

The advantages and the benefits of diversity in the workplace are not without challenges and include:

- ➢ Variance in cultures
- ➢ Accent
- ➢ Avoiding confusion
- ➢ Overcome morale problems
- ➢ Enable Team holds together
- ➢ Ideas solicitation from all
- ➢ Reward appropriately for solicited ideas

DIVERSITY WORKPLACE PROBLEM DATA (HIDDEN CURRICULUM)

An open curriculum through an organizational learning system is an innovation for achieving a successful diversity working environment. Because of the power in the knowledge of technology, some systems may attempt to discriminate training opportunities between diverse workforce. Human resources accountability for inclusion metrics should include transparency with projection to show openness. A barrier of diversity inclusion takes on various forms to awareness of decision-makers in the organization. The data about the existing workforce to accept diversity must not be ignored in getting the support needed in finding a solution to inclusion barriers. The availability of data can support a redesign of strategy for accommodation. An example is the larger organizations as federal agencies, states, and corporations, which depend on a real-time organizational performance through diversity Teams, and need a regular update for supporting consistency. An open curriculum through an organizational learning system is an innovation for achieving a successful diversity working environment. Because of the power in the knowledge of technology, some systems may attempt to discriminate training opportunities between diverse workforce. Human resources accountability for inclusion metrics should include transparency with projection to show openness. A barrier of diversity inclusion takes on various forms to awareness of decision-makers in the organization. The data about the existing workforce to accept diversity must not be ignored in getting the support needed in finding a solution to inclusion barriers. The availability of data can support a redesign of strategy for accommodation. An example is the larger organizations as federal agencies, states, and corporations, which depend on a real-time organizational performance through diversity Teams, and need a regular update for supporting consistency. An open curriculum through an organizational learning system is an innovation for achieving a successful diversity working environment. Because of the power in the knowledge of technology, some systems may attempt to discriminate training opportunities between diverse workforce. Human resources accountability for inclusion metrics should include transparency with projection to show openness. A barrier of diversity inclusion takes on various forms to awareness of decision-makers in the organization. The data about the existing workforce to accept diversity must not be ignored in getting the support needed in finding a solution to inclusion barriers. The availability of data can support a redesign of strategy for accommodation. An example is the larger organizations as federal agencies, states, and corporations, which depend on a real-time organizational performance through diversity Teams, and need a regular update for supporting consistency.

OUT GROUP WORKFORCE PLUS IN GROUP WORKFORCE = DIVERSITY

The equation constitutes the workforce from local and external sources involved with diversity workplace. Some recommendations for evaluating diversity workforce success through Formative and summative evaluation for:

➢ Satisfaction
➢ Diversity Agreement
➢ Quantitative obstacles

DIVERSITY IN THE WORKPLACE PLANNING

➢ planning for change
➢ Identify the area for change
➢ Area of agreement for change

Some organizations may have a formal diversity human capital plan in place to address problems of efficiency and enable productivity in a diverse workforce. For some organizations as the State, federal, charities, and corporations, a formal plan for diversity workforce integration is challenged, and may not achieve desired integration timely for various reasons.

CAUTION ABOUT DIVERSITY PLAN IMPLEMENTATION

➢ Diversity savvy executive
➢ Non bullying executive
➢ Team leadership intercultural competence
➢ Winning culture diversity spirit decorum

A person hired for D&I plan implementation may find it a challenge because of the internal complexity of the organization; therefore, the engagement of stakeholders becomes part of the solution.

SOME ANTICIPATED BENEFITS OF SUCCESSFUL DIVERSITY WORKFORCE-ETHICS

The hindrance of diversity is identified and acknowledged by the understanding of the meaning and effect on the organization including:

➢ Increased diversity members including foreign-born in leadership roles
➢ Consumerism of goods and services produced by diversity workforce promotes economic integration
➢ A competitive workforce with maximum utilization of labor force for the greater good of the economy to remain competitive in the world.
➢ The need to change from the high employee turnover rate owing to EAW (employment At-Will), based on culture, and promote diversity workforce inclusion and discourage organizational costs owing to high turnover.
➢ Harnessing and maximizing the utilization of the rich human resources in diversity workforce
➢ Promote the culture of no tolerance for xenophobia

ETHICS

To overcome the barriers to diversity inclusion requires increasing minorities' representation at leadership levels, including on the corporate boards, and balancing of diverse workforce management leadership structure to prevent single ethnic group dominance in public and private entities. In the banking and other industries in recent times, billions of dollars in investments were misdirected by individuals who could have avoided it by a diverse workforce balance. The misfortunes may have partly attributed to organizational leadership structural imbalance. The team leader needs an understanding of communication to increase efficiency across Team members. Team learning, therefore, extends to governmental, non-governmental organizations, and corporations to think insightfully and innovatively. Diversity workforce qualified diverse citizens can make a difference by contributing to organizational management security through leadership decisions.

A leadership structure to promote transparency for inclusion will involve a diverse board for preventing incidents like accounting book-cooking, owing to single ethnic dominance in authority. A diverse society will reflect the characteristics of rational inclusion. For example, accounting books cooking is among governmental, corporations including nonprofits, and detrimental to Investors and Taxpayers. A balanced diversity workforce can benefit stakeholders in several ways, but increasing the rate of diversity members on corporate boards is changing the dynamics, to reflect the reality. In less than fifty years the US as an example may have no dominant ethnicity. Besides investment security, the workforce can have high protection from ethnic dominant leadership organizational fraud risk (EDLOFR), as witnessed in recent decades. An example is the control of assets by single ethnic group members in the large organization, which may risk the investment to manipulation. The distribution of responsibilities among diverse groups can provide security for operational health. In banking practices as an example, the distribution of the vault combination key codes among managers from diverse groups is a lesson to learn. As a risk control measure, it is uncommon for a single manager of a bank to keep all the secret combination codes of the vault keys.

DIVERSITY INCLUSION (D&I) AND HYPOCRISY

"So we must think through what management should be accountable for; and how and through whom its accountability can be discharged. The stakeholders' interest both short and long-term, is one of the areas. But it is only one -Peter Drucker"

Bullying is among the barriers in societies, and controversial in schools, the Internet, and workplaces in the US. Bullying is less pronounced at workplaces than schools. The world's bullying organization has revealed that some leaders are part of the workplace bullying. Administrative directors or leaders will need to refrain from bullying diversity inclusion policy and avoid hypocrisy. Hypocrisy among organizations from governmental, nongovernmental, and corporations is common from the view of D&I success over the years. Honesty about inclusion remains a problem for authentic intercultural competent leadership. Research has revealed the rate for hypocrisy, nepotism, dishonesty, promise deception in promise-keeping, and disrespectfulness among leaders. For D& I to hold in an organization, it needs a guide with a code of conduct, minimizing subjective administrative judgment. Ethics to Guide the Plan among organizations from governmental, nongovernmental, and for-profits look at fairness for the success from various levels of organizational structures. Honesty remains a problem for Leadership competencies.

The diversity environment continues to show increasing Foreign-born population in the United States over the past decades, as one in nine Americans is born abroad. The quest for inclusion and the silence about hypocrisy about inclusion among some agencies towards remains a challenge for identifying obstacles and prospects for a solution. Americans are alert to workplace bullying and have experienced some abuses at workplaces involving women. Also, up to 90% of respondents in the study supported healthy workplace bills before the outbreak of sex abuses before the alarm from the Hollywood narrative about workplace practices involving females (worldbullying.org, 2014).

HOW DOES STAKEHOLDER ANALYSIS BENEFITS ORGANIZATION

Stakeholders' analysis will identify primary and secondary members with an interest in diversity in the organization. It also identified their common interests and potential power. The organization may not have all the answers for diversity inclusion as Afro-centric, Latinos, LGTB, or Jews communities among the diverse workforce but will allow the voices of employees to be held during policy decisions to prevent exclusion.

WHY ARE STAKEHOLDERS IMPORTANT

Stakeholders, as employees involved in a diversity inclusion plan, can contribute to the identification of potential conflicts or risks that could jeopardize organizational planning Opportunities. Employees should get involved at various stages of the organizational structure, to allow dialogic consultation for partnership in information gathering.

DIVERSITY INCLUSION STAKEHOLDERS

Stakeholders for a diversity inclusion strategy in the complex organization are those to benefit from the inclusion strategy, whose participation and support are crucial to the success of the inclusion plan.

ACCOUNTABILITY

Accountability for HCSP is important for success of organizational leadership. Ethical principles hold a view about openness for integrity in fostering the plan for achieving an equitable result. The political environment may become interactive, with increased minorities in leadership roles. A diversity inclusion plan will, therefore, emphasize honest responsibility. The solution to the success of human capital alignment is accountability by appropriate leaders responsible. Accountability needs principles for supporting periodic reviews for consistency with applicable Laws, as the gaps can cause unnecessary deviation from the direction, and impede the process of delivery for efficient services by the organization. Fundamental to organizational D&I transparency is accountability through the leadership traits, including; performance evaluation, and how leadership recognizes the implementation of diversity policy by measuring the progress in the organization. Former US vice president Al Gore's national partnership for reinventing government benchmarking study attributed accountability for diversity inclusion implementation among agencies for transparency (Gore, 2000).

> *"A key element to ensuring the success of any organizational initiative—especially diversity Initiatives—are accountability. Accountability is achieved by making the appropriate leaders responsible for diversity by linking performance evaluation elements and compensation to the successful implementation and progress of these initiatives. Accountability helps to ensure that "everyone is on board" and actively engaged in the diversity process." (U.S. department of commerce and vice president al gore's national partnership for reinventing government benchmarking study (Gore, 2000.)"*

DIVERSITY INCLUSION PLAN TEMPLATE

For effective inclusion in a large organization, an alignment plan will have an established protocol like one designed for federal agencies by the OPM. For an ordinary organization, a single model can serve the purpose.

THE NEED FOR SPECIFIC PLAN OF ACTION FOR D&I

The plan for D&I will include an internal timetable for adhering to standing laws, with a format describing how, when, and the effect on inclusion. The plan must identify the barriers, and how to evaluate them and educate the workforce on removing them over a period. An Alignment strategic human capital plan will involve collaborating through special initiatives by stakeholders for successful plan implementation across the organization.

POSIBLE DIVERSITY INCLUSION PLAN TEMPLATE

Diversity inclusion is controversial for a complex organizational system, owing to multifaceted approaches. A global template has become an example for agencies to develop their internal plans, using the protocol as the OPM designed model. Deviation from the template can cause complications for overcoming barriers. An organization will have a uniformed template and protocol to achieve the desired outcome.

LEARNING ORGANIZATIONAL ACCOUNTABILITY FOR EFFICIENCY AND ACCOUNTABILITY

Inclusion plan
The Generic Timetable sampling Structure:

- ❖ Timetable
- ❖ Collaboration
- ❖ Barriers Identification
- ❖ Elimination structure
- ❖ Special training for barriers identified
- ❖ Education about barriers avoidance
- ❖ Projection for Problem target elimination schedule
- ❖ Flexibility
- ❖ Fairness in rewards
- ❖ Collaboration with Minorities
- ❖ Leadership Intercultural Education
- ❖ Accountability for D&I
- ❖ Ethics& Bullying policy
- ❖ Measurability
- ❖ Federal Civilian Labor Force (FCLF)
- ❖ Workforce Percentages
- ❖ Workforce Distribution by Race and National Origin Percentages
- ❖ Workforce Distribution by Minorities and Women
- ❖ Federal and Relevant Civilian Labor Workforce
- ❖ Supervisory vs. Non supervisory Workforce
- ❖ Distribution of women and minorities in executive level positions
- ❖ Mission Critical Occupational (MCO) Representation Gender race and National Origin(OPM, 2017)

SAMPLING STRUCTURE OF (D & I) PLAN IMPLEMENTING OFFICE

- ❖ Certification that a plan exists at agency
- ❖ Structure of office responsible for D&I plan
- ❖ Planning and implementation
- ❖ Recommendation
- ❖ Communicating the plan to agency
- ❖ Reports
- ❖ Underrepresented hiring
- ❖ Recruitment for diversity applicants
- ❖ Barrier elimination strategy
- ❖ OPM update
- ❖ D&I plan hiring system
- ❖ Advisory service for all selection for employment
- ❖ Evaluate the knowledge of minorities' education (OPM, 2017).

THE PROPONENTS OF THE BALANCED SCORECARD (BSC)

The proponents of the balanced scorecard (BSC), including David Norton and John Kaplan, advanced the method for the measurement of an effective organization as a learning methodology, with attention on customer services, financial management, internal organizational behavior, and how to improve organizational growth (Kaplan& Norton, 1992). The culture of an organization can affect the strategy for achieving high-level performance to realize growth desires by changing the culture, which must begin with the leader to the lower levels of power.   A balanced scorecard is a tool used for supporting management in planning for improving the operational and administrative services, including human capital problems, involving inclusion to balance the workforce operational health, for efficiency and productivity for organizational growth.

The balancing of diversity workplace through strategic planning can result in achieving the desired change in human capital. The tool can help an organization with planning to overcome organizational developmental challenges and track the execution of the strategic plan through monitoring and control, to ensure its implementation. The number of executive orders from the Whitehouse in recent decades by respective presidents about diversity inclusion in the US is evident for reinforcement. Agencies' Leadership will power to implement orders for inclusion remains political. The willingness to improve on diversity inclusion can anticipate overcoming the barriers, including intercultural competence leadership. The principles of ethics hold a view about openness for fostering a plan for achieving an equitable result on issues involving diversity inclusion. A human capital inclusion plan will openly identify the barriers connected with productivity connected with a balanced diversity workforce. An unbalanced diversity workforce can affect productivity and efficiency.

TABLE T: BAC SAMPLE MAP FOR NONPROFIT HCSP MODEL

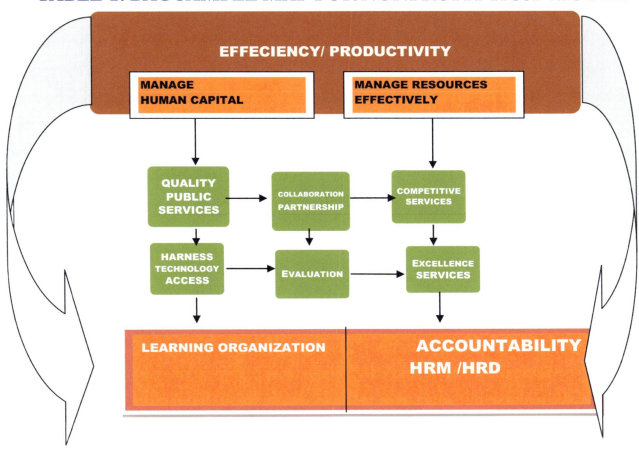

jfseekie©2019

THE ALTERNATIVE SCORE CARD STRATEGY FOR EFFFICIENCY FOR PRODUCTIVITY SHOWS HOW MANAGING HUMAN CAPITAL AND NON HUMAN CAPITAL RESOURCES TO ACHIEVE LEARNING ORGANIZATIONAL ACCOUNTABILITY FOR EFFICIENCY AND PRODUCTIVITY.

DESKILLING AND RESKILLING

Deskilling and Reskilling for governmental and nongovernmental Organizations have become fundamental at various levels of the economy. During the transitional period to a knowledge-based economy driven by technology, advancing capacity building is resourceful for solving organizational deficiency. Overcoming barriers in financial and human capital management can support workforce sustainability. The mandate for inclusion is coded with terminologies to decode. Critics about intercultural competence remain critical about organizations locally and globally, to eliminate constraints in achieving cognitive-based knowledge.

CULTURAL DIALOGUE

Cultural dialogue is critical for addressing cultural intelligence and competence learning for understanding diversity Workforce. Diversity literature is evolving, and continuing education is one best way to learn it in organizations. The technology gap Bridging (TGB), can remain updated by elevating information and education, across organizations through collaborative learning. Issues may include (one), leadership structure (two), intercultural knowledge gap (ICKG), technology gap Bridging (TG), and (three), Deskilling and Reskilling (D&R). Organizations will engage a plan that addresses issues including leadership deficit, and Gender parity index (GPI), with a logic model for overcoming diversity inclusion barriers.

ROLE OF BOARD IN STRATEGIC PLANNING

A strategic planning board (SPB) is a special board from a regular organizational board and is engaged in monitoring of the plan. The board will monitor the implementation for consistency in achieving the goals of the plan. Employees' inclusion will involve affinities and opportunities during the implementation, and the neutrality of managers in implementing the plan for a fairer distribution of opportunities is assured. The goal of the plan will focus on creating a balanced workforce environment and will have a specified timetable, like over a quadrennial period and continuity. The purpose of the board is to support the implementation for the success of the plan during the process. Stakeholder analysis holds a view about the treatment of members from being ambiguous. The confusion about stakeholder analysis theory from distortion remains a challenge. The ambiguity of affinities inclusion can affect the outcome of the SP when the projection with clarification is not measurable and clear. The implementing managers and directors may not be decision-makers for designing the plan, and simultaneously implementing it, fearing accountability, usually not without fusses among organizations. The absence of the check and balance can become faulty. The decisional template must be opened and controlled to avoid the repeat of the status quo. The board will make sure the purpose of SP for the organization is maintained, closing the gaps of under representation of affinities in leadership roles, technology, and among other opportunities. For a complex organization, stakeholders may include internal and external groups with a shared interest.

SP may involve a shift in the structure of human resources, including leadership ranks, and the chances of protecting the plan from being undermined from a cascading effect. Human resources have a role in changing dynamics for a strategic inclusion plan focused on human capital inclusion. The role of the board, for complex organization, will include frequent interactions with the group responsible for the plan's management to identify and resolve issues for adjustment. In a system like the US with Affirmative Action subtle laws, compounded with D&I in the global context, the challenge is immense and needs an intercultural competent leadership to drive the change effectively. Balancing between the status quo's culture, and the realism that inclusion demands, remains the challenge.

WHAT METRIC

The metric for overcoming diversity inclusion leadership and skills deficit among organizations will involve strategic planning for filling the gaps in knowledge, inconsistencies, conflicts, and intercultural competent management (ICM) to support the policies. The uniform application of the inclusion plan by agencies such as under an alignment system will avoid delays by sub-agencies in the case as the federal system, from interpreting D&I differently, including its definition. A system will maintain consistency, consciousness, and resilience through strategic planning as a tool for measuring and sustaining diversity workforce integration.

CONCLUSION

The role of Team leadership, as analyzed in this book, can contribute to the successful diversity of human capital inclusion plan. A strategic plan may vary in problem-solving among industries during the transition from the life cycle of organizational existence to another. The deficit of intercultural competence leadership in contemporary organizational development involving diversity inclusion has the potential to undermine efficiency. It needs guidance to maintain an operational equilibrium. Diversity inclusion value will recognize citizenship, accommodation, and global etiquette to advance globalization demands of the greater number for the greater good.

ACRONYMS

ADIB =ASSOCIATED DIVERSITY INCLUSION BARRIERS

AHCS= ALIGNMENT HUMAN CAPITAL STRATEGIC PLANNING

BSC= BALANCE SCORE CARD

BWE=BALANCED WORKFORCE ENVIRONMENT

AUM=ANXIETY /UNCERTAINTY MANAGEMENT THEORY

CAT=COMMUNICATION AND ACCOMMODATION

CASSW= CANADIAN ASSOCIATION OF SCHOOLS OF SOCIAL WORK

ACCU=ASSOCIATION OF AMERICAN COLLEGES AND UNIVERSITIES

D&I =DIVERSITY INCLUSION

DITF= DIVERSITY TEAM INTEGRATED FORMING

DCE=DIVERSITY CULTURAL ENVIRONMENT

DTIA =DIVERSITY INTEGRATED TEAM ACCLIMATING

DTID =DIVERSITY TEAM INTEGRATED DEVELOPING

DTIH =DIVERSITY INTEGRATED HARMONIZING

DTIPC =DIVERSITY TEAM INTEGRATED PRACTICING AND COACHING

DTL= DIVERSITY TEAM LEADERSHIP

DCE=DIVERSITY CULTURAL ENVIRONMENT

EU= EUROPEAN UNION

EGAA=EQUAL GENDA AFFIRMATIVE ACTION

FCLF=FEDERAL CIVILIAN LABOR FORCE

EDLOFR= ETHNIC DOMINANTS LEADERSHIP ORGANIZATIONAL FRAUD RISK

GGI = GENDER GAP INDEX

GPI=GENDER PARITY INDEX

HPD= HIGH POWER DISTANCE CULTURE

HP=HIGH POWERED

HR =HUMAN RESOURCES

HRD=HUMAN RESOURCE DEVELOPMENT

HTM=HARDNOSED TEAM MEMBERS

HRM= HUMAN RESOURCE MANAGEMENT

ICKG= INTER CULTURAL KNOWLEDGE GAP

ICCD= INTERCULTURAL COMPETENCE DEFICIT

ICM=INTERCULTURAL COMPETENT MANAGEMENT

L&INGOS=LOCAL AND INTERNATIONAL NON GOVERNMENTAL ORGANIZATIONS

LPD=LOW POWER DISTANCE CULTURE

LGTB=LESBIAN GAY TRANS-GENDER

MCO=MISSION CRITICAL OCCUPATION

MD= MANAGEMENT DIRECTIVE (MD715

NAFTA=NORTH AMERICA FREE TRADE

NFOC= NEED FOR ORGANIZATIONAL CHANGE

NRP= NATURAL RATIONAL PHENOMENON

OMS =ORGANIZATIONAL MOTIVATIONAL STRATEGIES

OPM =OFFICE OF PERSONNEL MANAGEMENT

POCAIE = PLANNING, ORGANIZING, COORDINATING, ADAPTING, IMPLEMENTING AND EVALUATING

POOR=POTENTIAL ORGANIZATIONAL RISK

PSP=PERSONAL SKILL PROFICIENCY (PSP)

SDL=SELF- DIRECTED LEARNING

SP =STRATEGIC PLANNING

SQS= STATUS QUO SYNDROME

SWOT=STRENGTH WEAKNESSES OPPORTUNITY THREAT

TUS-TRANS- UNCONSCIOUSNESS SYNDROME

TGB=TECHNOLOGY GAP BRIDGING

UCA=UNCERTAINTY AVOIDANCE

UB=UNCONSCIOUS BIAS

USAID=UNITED STATES AGENCY FOR INTERNATIONAL DEVELOPMENT

BE=BALANCED WORKFORCE ENVIRONMENT

WFIC= WORKFORCE MANAGEMENT INTERCULTURAL
COMPETENCE

INDEX

ABOUT AUTHOR

JAMES F. S. SEEKIE, Sr.
EDUCATION
LEARNER PHD USA
MA (INTERNATIONAL BUSINESS), USA
BANKING STUDIES, EUROPEAN UNION
WORK EXPERIENCE
STATE AND FEDERAL GOVERNMENT FINANCIAL OPERATIONS
BANKING AND GLOBAL CORPORATIONS
GLOBAL INTERNATIONAL NON PROFITS MANAGEMENT
FINANCIAL CONTROLLER, PUBLIC FINANCE
PRODUCER -BANKING JOURNAL
COMMUNITY COMMISSIONER AFRICAN AMERICAN MEN COMMISSION - MINNESOTA
INTERNSHIPS
INTERNATIONAL BUSINESS STUDIES: NAFTA-CANADIAN
MINISTRY OF FOREIGN AFFAIRS, MONTREAL CANADA
EUROPEAN UNION TRADE RELATION WITH
AFRICAN CARIBBEAN AND THE PACIFIC'S (ACPS)
WORLD BANK, US AGENCY FOR INTERNATIONAL
DEVELOPMENT (USAID) UNITED NATIONS
INTERNATIONAL MONETARY FUND (IMF) WASHINGTON DC
INTERNATIONAL TRADE FAIR EUROPEAN UNION

BIBLIOGRAPHY

Allan, Blake A. Tebbe, Elliot A. Duffy, Ryan, D. Autin, Kelsey L. (2015).*Career Development Quarterly.* https://onlinelibrary.wiley.com/doi/abs/10.1002/cdq.12030

Allison, M., & Kaye, J. (2005). Strategic planning for nonprofit organizations: A practical Guide and workbook (2nd Edition) Hoboken, N.J. USA. John Wiley & Sons

Allport, G. W. (1954). The nature of prejudice. Cambridge, MA: Perseus Books

Association of American Colleges and Universities & Claremont Graduate University. (2002). Campus Diversity Initiative Evaluation Project: Campus Guidelines for Creating an Evaluation Plan. Available at:http://www.aacu.org/irvinediveval/pdfs/Campus_Guidelines.pdf

Avakoli, M. (2015). Diversity & inclusion drive success for today's leaders. TD: *Talent Development*, 69(5), 46-51.

Avey, J. B., Wernsing, T. S. & Palanski, M. E. (2012). Exploring the Process of Ethical Leadership: The Mediating Role of Employee Voice and Psychological Ownership. *Journal of Business Ethics, 107*(1), 21–34.https://academic.microsoft.com/paper/90970949/citedby/search?q=An%20integrative%2

Avolio, B. J., Walumbwa, F. O., & Weber, T. J. (2009). Leadership: Current Theories, Research, and Future Directions. *Annual Review of Psychology, 60*(1), 421–449.https://academic.microsoft.com/paper/90970949/citedby/search?q=An%20integrative%2

Avolio, Bruce J. (2007). "Promoting more integrative strategies for leadership theory-building". American Psychologist. 62 (1): 25–33. *CiteSeerX 10.1.1.467.7223*. *doi*:*10.1037/0003-066x.62.1.25*. *PMID 17209677*.

Beers, SJ, P. (2009). *An introduction to Bernard Lonergan., Exploring Lonergan's approach to the great philosophical questions.* Victoria, Australia. Sid Harta Publishers, Ltd.

Boudreaux, M., Bowen, A. Thom A, R. (2012), Skills for Diversity and Inclusion in Organizations: A Review and Preliminary Investigation.*Psychologist-Manager Journal*, 15: 128–141, 2012

Bryson, J. M., & Alston, F. K. (2011). Creating your strategic plan: A workbook for public and Nonprofit organizations (3rd Ed.). San Francisco, CA: Jossey-Bass.

Canadian Association of Schools of Social Work (2004). The Challenge of Diversity, Canadian Association of Schools of Social Work, Ottawa. CASSW Standards for Accreditation, Canadian Association of Schools of Social Work, Ottawa Commission for Higher Education, Boulder. http://www.cassw-acess.ca/

Carr-Ruffino, N. (2013). Managing diversity (9th ed.). Boston, MA: Pearson Learning Solutions.

Carson, Charles (Spring 2018). "A historical view of Douglas McGregor's Theory Y". Journal of Management Decision. 43 (3): 450–460. https://www.emerald.com/insight/content/doi/10.1108/00251740510589814/full/html

Carter, J. W. M. (2016). Whren's Flawed Assumptions Regarding Race, History, and Unconscious Bias. *Case Western Reserve Law Review*, 66(4), 947–956.

Cervone, H. F. (2014). Improving Strategic Planning by Adapting Agile Methods to the Planning Process. *Journal of Library Administration*, *54*(2), 155–168.

Ciulla, J.B., Murphy, S.E., & Price, T.L. (2005). *The quest for moral leaders: Essays on leadership Essays on Leadership Ethics.* Cheltenham, UK Northampton, MA, USA

Daft, R. L & Marcic, D. (2006) 5th ed. Understanding management, Thomson Corporation press, OH.USA

Dervitsiotis, K. N. (2001). Looking at the whole picture in performance improvement programmes. *Total Quality Management, 12*(6), 687–700.

Donaldson, T., & Preston, L. E. 1995. corporation concept, evidence, and implications .The stakeholder theory of the corporation. *Academy of Management Review* (20) 65–91.

Dykstra, k. (2018). Defeat Unconscious Bias through Manager Training. *TD: Talent Development, 72*(7), 70–71.

Ellerman, D. (2001). McGregor's Theory Y vs. Bentham's Panopticism: Toward a Critique of the Economic Theory of Agency. *Knowledge, Technology & Policy, 14*(1), 34.

Esaiasson, P., & Gilljam, M. Kokkonen, A., (2015). Diverse Workplaces and Interethnic Friendship Formation—A Multilevel Comparison across 21 OECD Countries. Journal of Ethnic & Migration Studies, 41(2), 284-305. doi:10.1080/1369183X.2014.902300

European Union. (2010) Annual report 2009.Retrieved January 16, 2011, from http://www.EU.Org.

EEOC.Gov. (2019).Equal employment opportunity commission. Equal employment opportunity management directive md-715https://www.eeoc.gov/federal/directives/md715.cfm

Federal Register. (2017).establishing a coordinated government wide initiative to promote diversity and inclusion in the federal Government.https://www.federalregister.gov/documents/2011/08/23/2011-21704/establishing-a-coordinated-government-wide-initiative-to-promote-diversity-and-inclusion-in-the

Fiarman, S. E. (2016). Unconscious Bias. *Educational Leadership, 74*(3), 10–15.

Ghumman, S., Ryan, A. M., Barclay, L. A., & Markel, K. S. (2013). Religious Discrimination in the Workplace: A Review and Examination of Current and Future Trends.

Journal of Business and Psychology, *28*(4), 439–454.https://academic.microsoft.com/paper/90970949/citedby/search?q=An%20integrative%2

Giles, Howard, Reid, Scott, Harwood& Jake (2010). Communication. New York: Peter Lang. p. 319.ISBN 978-1-4331-0398-8.

Gore, A(2000). National Partnership for Reinventing Government (U.S.). (2000). Best practices in achieving workforce diversity: U.S. Department of Commerce and Vice President Al Gore's national partnership for reinventing government benchmarking study. Washington, D.C.: U.S. Dept. of Commerce.

Graf, S. Paolini, S. Rubin, M. (2014). "Negative intergroup contact is more influential, but positive intergroup contact is more common: Assessing contact prominence and contact prevalence in five Central European countries". European Journal of Social Psychology. 44 (6): 536–547. doi:10.1002/ejsp.2052.

Gudykunst, William B. (2005, William B. (2005). Theorizing About Intercultural Communication. Thousand Oaks: SAGE Publications, Inc. pp. viii. ISBN 9780761927495.

Hattangadi, V. (2015). Theory X & Theory Y. *International Journal of Recent Research Aspects*, *2*(4), 20–21.

Hofstede, Geert (2001). Culture's Consequences: comparing values, behaviors, institutions, and organizations across nations (2nd ed.). Thousand Oaks, CA: *SAGE Publications*. *ISBN 978-0-8039-7323-7*.

Indiana University–Purdue University Indianapolis (2001) .Diversity Performance Indicators. Available at: http://www.iport.iupui.edu/performance/perf_diversity.htm

Jensen, B. (2006). 640,000 New Senior Managers Will Be Needed to Run Nonprofit Groups in Next Decade. Chronicle of Philanthropy, 18(12), 46 https://www.philanthropy.com/specialreport/philanthropy-400-a-new-no-1/111

Johnson-Laird, P. N. (2010). "Mental models and human reasoning". Proceedings of the National Academy of Sciences. 107. pp. 18243–18250. Doi: 10.1073/pnas.1012933107. *https://www.pnas.org/content/pnas/early/2010/10/11/1012933107.full.pdf*

Johnston, W. B. (1987). Workforce 2000: Work and workers for the 21st century. *Hudson Institute.* http://files.eric.ed.gov/fulltext/ED290887.pdf

Kaplan, R. S., Norton, D. P. (1992). "The Balanced Scorecard—Measures That Drive Performance," *Harvard Business Review,* January–February 1992, p. 71–79

Kim, Y. J., & Van Dyne, L. (2012). Cultural Intelligence and International Leadership Potential: The Importance of Contact for Members of the Majority. Applied Psychology: An International Review, 61(2), 272–294. HTTPS://WWW.RESEARCHGATE.NET/PUBLICATION/229920957_ DO - 10.1111/j.1464-0597.2011.00468.

Lett, H (1945). "Techniques for achieving interracial cooperation". Proceedings of the Institute on Race Relations and Community Organization. Chicago: University of Chicago and the American Council on Race Relations.

Mazziotta, A.; Mummendey, A.; Wright, C. S. (2011). "Vicarious intergroup contact effects: Applying social-cognitive theory to intergroup contact research". Group Processes & Intergroup Relations. 14 (2): 255–274. Doi: 10.1177/1368430210390533.

Mintzberg, Henry; Quinn, James B. (1996). The Strategy Process: Concepts, Contexts, Cases. Prentice Hall. ISBN 978-0-132-340304.

Mone, I. S., Benga, O., & Opre, A. (2016). Cross-Cultural Differences in Socialization Goals as a Function of Power Distance, Individualism-Collectivism and Education. *Romanian*

Journal of Experimental Applied Psychology, 7, 330–334. https://www.researchgate.net/publication/307990807

Northhouse, P.G. (2007).Leadership Theory and Practice. (Fourth edition). Sage publications, California Publishers, Ltd.

Office of personnel Management (2016). Government wide Inclusive Diversity Strategic Plan. Retrieved from: https://www.usa.gov/federal-agencies/office-of-p

Parham,W.D.(Jan.2015).Journal of Multicultural Counseling and Development: Second Special Issue on Diversity and Inclusion in Higher Education. *Journal of Multicultural Counseling and Development . January 2015 • Vol. 43.*

Pettigrew, T. F. Tropp, L. R. (2006). "A meta-analytic test of intergroup contact theory". Journal of Personality and Social Psychology. 90 (5): 751–783. doi:10.1037/0022-3514.90.5.751.

Philip,N. J.L(2010). Mental models and human reasoning. Proceedings of the National Academy of Sciences Oct 2010, 107 (43) 18243-18250; DOI: 10.1073/pnas.1012933107

Porter & Kramer (corporate social responsibility" Harvard Business review," *making a real difference" retrieved 08/17/2007*

Rhine, A. S. (2015). An Examination of the Perceptions of Stakeholders on Authentic Leadership in Strategic Planning in Nonprofit Arts Organizations. *Journal of Arts Management, Law & Society, 45*(1), 3–21.

Rubin, M.; Sibley, C. G. (2012). "The contact caveat: Negative contact predicts increased prejudice more than positive contact predicts reduced prejudice". Personality and Social Psychology Bulletin. 38 (12): 1629–1643. doi:10.1177/0146167212457953.

Simmons, C., Clemons, J. G., & Bennett, C. B. (2003). Does Your Company Discriminate? *Black Enterprise, 33*(12), 80.

Tajfel, H., & Turner, J. (2001). An integrative theory of intergroup conflict. *The Social Psychology of Intergroup Relations*.https://academic.microsoft.com/paper/90970949/citedby/search?q=An%20integrative%2

Thomas, D. R. (2001). Communication in personal relationships across cultures Gudykunst WB, Ting-Toomey S, & Nishida T. (eds) (1996) Sage, Thousand Oaks, CA: 268 pp., 24.00 ISBN 0-8039-4672-4 (paperback).

Tucker, B. (2010). Through Which Lens. Contingency and Institutional Approaches to Conceptualizing Organizational Performance in the Not-for-Profit Sector. *Journal of Applied Management Accounting Research*, 8(1), 17-33.

Tuckman, B.W. (1965). Developmental sequences in small groups. *Psychological Bulletin, 63*, 384-399.

Unnever, J.D. (2016).The impact of Immigration on Iindicators of the well-being of the Black Population in the United States. *The western journal of Black Studies, vol.40 (1)*

White, F. A., Abu-Rayya, H. Weitzel, C. (2014). "Achieving twelve-months of intergroup bias reduction: The dual identity-electronic contact (DIEC) experiment". International Journal of Intercultural Relations. 38: 158–163. Doi: 10.1016/j.ijintrel.2013.08.002.

World Bullying Institute. (2017). The 2014 WBI US workplace bullying survey. http://www.workplacebullying.org/2014-rank/

Yang ji, Erhua Zhou, Caiyun li, & Yanling Yan. (2015). Power Distance Orientation and Employee Help Seeking: Trust in Supervisor as a Mediator. Social Behavior & Personality: *An International Journal*, 43(6) 1043–1054.

Printed in the United States
By Bookmasters